Your Towns and Cities in the Great War

Washington
in the Great War

Peter Welsh.

Your Towns and Cities in the Great War

Washington
in the Great War

'Whisht Lads'

Peter Welsh

Pen & Sword
MILITARY

First published in Great Britain in 2014 by
PEN & SWORD MILITARY
an imprint of
Pen and Sword Books Ltd
47 Church Street
Barnsley
South Yorkshire S70 2AS

Copyright © Peter Welsh, 2014

ISBN 978 1 78346 385 5

The right of Peter Welsh to be identified as the author of
this work has been asserted by him in accordance with the Copyright,
Designs and Patents Act 1988.

A CIP record for this book is available from the British Library

Printed and bound in England by Page Bros, Norwich.

Typeset in Times New Roman by Chic Graphics

Pen & Sword Books Ltd incorporates the imprints of
Pen & Sword Archaeology, Atlas, Aviation, Battleground, Discovery,
Family History, History, Maritime, Military, Naval, Politics, Railways,
Select, Social History, Transport, True Crime, Claymore Press,
Frontline Books, Leo Cooper, Praetorian Press, Remember When,
Seaforth Publishing and Wharncliffe.

For a complete list of Pen and Sword titles please contact
Pen and Sword Books Limited
47 Church Street, Barnsley, South Yorkshire, S70 2AS, England
E-mail: enquiries@pen-and-sword.co.uk
Website: www.pen-and-sword.co.uk

Contents

Acknowledgements   7

Introduction   8

1   Washington, Harraton and Usworth pre-war   10

2   War Comes   16

3   First Casualties   29

4   Well we don't want to lose you… but we'll be proud of you if you go   34

5   1915… Summary: Bother at the Bridge, Tribunals, Gallipoli, Loos   40

6   What did you do in the war, Mammy?   55

7   1916…Summary: International Game, Sergeant Marsden writes home; disabled, discharged and deepest sympathy, Jutland, the Somme, casualties   64

8   1917…Summary: USA joins in, Belgian morality and rations, recipes and food orders, allotments, school strike, JW Cook's, casualties   79

9   1918…Summary: profiteering, potatoes, fish, casualties   102

10 The brave men living and dead….   113

11 For us the war is over   119

12 Homes for heroes   126

13 At the going down of the sun….   128

14 Set in Stone   138

15 Epitaph   147

     Addendum   153

     Appendices – Names on Usworth, Washington and
Harraton Memorials together with Regiments and dates
of death   154

     Index   168

Acknowledgements

This book would not have been possible without the support of Wessington U3A whose structures, and supportive members, have made possible our exhibitions and displays, applications for grants and general organisation.

I'd particularly like to thank Margaret Welsh, Gavin and Pauline Butterfield, Anne Phillipson, Liz Eddon, Tom Copeman, Ann Huntley, Wendy Eggerton, Barbara Fiddy and Gordon Fletcher – the Washington Pals' Battalion. 'Wad thou help?' 'Aa wad.'

Staff at Tyne and Wear Archives, Newcastle and Gateshead Libraries and Durham County Record Office have explained where the haystacks are and how we might find (or not) the needles hidden within. Local families have been, without exception, generous with their treasures and stories. Steve Jenkins of Leyton Orient Supporters' Club and author of *They Took the Lead* has provided support, advice and photographs of William Jonas. Helen Barker and Gemma Reed at Beamish Museum have helped with artefacts and advice. The Co-op Community Fund, North Biddick Social Club, Washington Community Development Fund, Washington History Society, Sir James Knott Trust, Sainsbury's at Washington, Gentoo and the Community Foundation have offered us grants for exhibitions. The North East War Memorials Project is an indispensable support. Sunderland City Council has offered support, both financial and moral. Gareth Crickmer at the *Washington Star* has helped us create a local profile and Mimi and Jackie Pillon at Varennes en Croix, Picardy, have provided us with wonderful lodgings and 'improve your French cos we don't speak much English' courses near the battlefields. Keith and Richard at Lab@dh3imaging.co.uk have supplied display boards of high quality.

So, thanks and well done to all the above. All errors are my responsibility. Apologies if there are any.

Introduction

This book had its origins in a study of the names on the South Hylton War Memorial, a pupil at Pennywell School having brought in a collection of documents from South Hylton British Legion Club that were 'going in the bin' if they could not find a home.

Our, that is the Fatfield and Harraton Chums' Battalion, first research effort was to identify the men named on the memorial to the 'brave men of Harraton Parish'. Then, with retirement and meeting like-minded people, it became a study of the memorials at Usworth (inside Holy Trinity Church), Washington Village and Fatfield and the formation of a group within the recently formed Wessington U3A. Just like Topsy…

If the question is, 'Wad thou gan?' then the answer is 'We wad' and so we've been to visit the graves and memorials of local men in Northern Italy, Berlin, Belgium, France, Gallipoli and the UK and there are still more to see, both at home and abroad.

Not only that, there are some men still not satisfactorily identified – the search goes on.

In researching such a topic it is impossible to separate the men from their families, homes, workplaces, attitudes and recreation – and the book attempts to give a view of what was happening in Washington during the Great War, as well as paying tribute to the men who were away fighting it and whose fates had such an impact on these three pit villages.

Local libraries and archives have been given files with what we know about the men (and one woman), who died as a result of their service, so if you, dear reader, want more information, it is available. Of course the files were out of date as soon as they were printed and new information has been obtained about some of the men, but that's life. In addition we have many photographs of men, their graves and various pieces of ephemera, all of the latter provided by relatives. All photographs and information can be supplied, by email, free of charge.

All names of men (and one woman) on the memorials at Fatfield, Washington and Usworth are emboldened in the text e.g., **Stephen Mills, Fred Armstrong**.

petewelshgettysburg@btinternet.com

Check out wwmp.weebly.com for links to our film *Washington Men in the Great War: "Wad thou gan? – Aye aa wad"*.

Photograph Credits

Where there is no source against the photograph – these are photographs freely available in and around the village. Thus Joan Nichol has a large number of photographs of old Washington, so too Jim Gill, so too Washington History Society. I'm aware that it's possible that some of the photographs could still have copyright attached but locating the copyright holder seems unlikely. Can I therefore apologise to anyone whose copyright has been infringed and state that it was not done with the intention of denying your rights.

CHAPTER 1

Washington, Harraton and Usworth Pre-war

Washington

Kelly's Directory of 1914 describes Washington thus, '…a parish, township and considerable village near the navigable river Wear…7 miles west from Sunderland, 7 south-east from Newcastle and 10 north-east from Durham, in the Chester-le-Street division of the county, in the ward and union of Chester-le-Street, petty sessional division and county court of Gateshead, rural deanery of Chester-le-Street and archdeaconry and diocese of Durham'.

Kelly's then featured Holy Trinity Church, a Catholic chapel, a Wesleyan chapel, and further Wesleyan, Primitive Methodist and Plymouth Brethren chapels at Washington Station. Dame Margaret's Hall, affiliated to Dr Barnardo's, was a home for waifs and strays. It mentions an extensive colliery [F Pit], an iron works [Cook's], a bath brick manufactory [Bowring & Co] and a Chemical Works [Newalls]. The chief landowners were the trustees of Robert Charles Duncombe Shafto, Wenman Aubrey Wykeham-Musgrave and Sir Wilfred Lawson, Bart. The area of the township was 1,973 acres, the main crops were wheat, barley, oats and turnips and the population of the township in 1911 was 7,821. *Kelly's* also listed significant people at New Washington and Washington Station, areas separate, but not far, from the old village. They included the normal range of butchers, bakers, candlestick makers, undertakers, publicans and grocers. Argentina was represented by the River Plate Meat Co., the medical profession by Doctors Farquharson, Tocher and Jacques and banking by Lloyds.

Close by was Barmston, a small township of 917 acres and a population of 492. Barmston had its own Parish Council whose concerns, as war approached, included the condition of the footpaths and roads between Victoria Bridge and Washington Chemical Works, how to get the North Eastern Railway Company to improve links with South Shields and subjects like street lighting (for which they paid Washington Chemical Works) and scavenging.

Harraton

Again, according to *Kelly's Directory* of 1914, 'Harraton is an Ecclesiastical Parish formed on 29 October 1875 from the parishes of Birtley and Chester-le-Street and including the hamlets and villages of Fatfield, Chatershaugh, North Biddick, Harraton, Nova Scotia, Pelaw and Picktree in the Chester-le-Street division of the county, Chester-le-Street petty sessions division and union, Durham County court district, rural deanery of Chester-le-Street and archdeaconry and diocese of Durham.' Phew, so many different nomenclatures, divisions and classifications. The entry went on, 'St George's, erected in 1879 at a cost of £5,000, defrayed by the Earl of Durham, is a red brick Gothic style structure; there are 320 sittings. The living is a Vicarage with a yearly value of £290, with residence, in the gift of the Earl of Durham and held, since 1879, by the Reverend William Samuel Reeman of St Bee's.'

'Harraton is a township chiefly co-extensive with the ecclesiastical parish of Fatfield.' Its population in 1911 was 3,399 i.e. including Fatfield's population of 2,956.

'North Biddick is a hamlet in which are the Worm Hill and Worm Well, principal spots connected with the legend of the Lambton Worm – the hill is an artificial mound of conical shape, the well twenty-six yards from the hill is now hardly traceable.'

As noted by *Kelly's,* the main people in the village of Fatfield were Mary Ann Archer – Dun Cow, Francis Carr – colliery engineer, Henry Carr – grocer and Post Office, Thomas Hall – farmer of Fatfield House, Harraton Colliery – manager G.W. Minto, Alexander Morris – farmer of Harraton Hall, J&H Oswald & Sons – boot and shoe makers, Edward Ranson – shopkeeper in Nova Scotia, Thomas Scott – head gamekeeper to Lord Lambton, John Todd – Ferryboat Inn and John Wilson – hairdresser.

Fatfield Village from the bridge.

James Falshaw Cook lived in Picktree House. Tyne and Wear Archives has details of a contract between, 'Bought of Maple', a London company which had furnished Picktree House for James Falshaw Cook. No date is given for the contract but it seems to have been in the first twenty years of the century. At a cost of £1091.10s.10d a full range of furnishings and decoration was supplied for 'Dining Room, Smoke Room, Own Bedroom 1, Dressing Room No 2, Spare Bedroom, 3 Bedrooms, Servants' Bedroom, Kitchen, Hall Landing and Vestibule.' The family paid a cheque for £591.10s.10d, leaving £500 to be paid later. The book in which the contract is detailed resonates like an episode of *Upstairs, Downstairs*.

At North Biddick: people of note included John J. Oxley – Biddick Hall, James Berriman – Biddick Inn, William Collins – Victoria Hotel, Fatfield and District Workmen's Club and Institute Union – William Lister, Secretary, George Emmerson Forster – North Biddick farm, Thomas E. James – Railway Tavern, Robert Lawson – beer retailer, Havelock Inn, North Biddick Colliery – manager R.C. Thomas, John Scott – newsagent, Thomas Smith – artificial teeth maker [later to seek exemption from military service], Frederick Tuck – Victoria Bridge Inn, Ernest William Walton – assistant overseer of 20, Wormhill Terrace, Henry Wilson – builder.

Kelly's doesn't mention John George Lambton, third Earl of Durham, other than in noting some of his possessions of land and buildings, but he lived nearby in Lambton Castle, technically in Fencehouses, and was the major figure in the area. Harraton and North Biddick collieries were both part of the group of sixteen collieries owned by the Lambton and Hetton Coal Company, Chairman Rt. Hon Lord Joicey of Ford Castle, Berwick-upon Tweed. Lord Joicey had bought the Lambton Collieries from Lord Durham in 1896 and he bought the Hetton Collieries from Sir Lindsay Wood in 1911. The main agent for this company was Austin Kirkup. The company employed 15,900 people in 1914.

On Whit Monday, May 1913, G.W. Minto, manager of Harraton Colliery, had formally opened the Recreation Ground. There were races for the lads and skipping contests for the girls – prizes paid for from the public collection of £1.17s.0d. The Parish Council had plans for five seats, four boats, a boat house and grappling irons, a bowling green, a man to be employed to oversee the area and a series of rules. When the council finally agreed on these there were the usual common sense ones and the usual 'what on earth?' examples of officialdom gone mad. Thus, people carrying large baskets or packages were not to be admitted and it was expressly forbidden to beat or shake carpets, druggetts (woollen or coarse woven fabric used as a covering), mats or rugs. 'The Rec' was normally open from 8 am–6 pm but in the summer this was extended to cover the hours 6 am to 10 pm. No vehicles other than perambulators and invalid carriages were allowed, nor were drunks; profane, indecent and offensive language was prohibited and so were gambling, the soliciting of alms, preaching of politics, religious demonstrations and walking on the flowerbeds. Smoking was not allowed in the buildings and refreshments were only to be sold from the rooms. Anyone breaking these rules could be fined up to 40s.

Harraton Parish Council, chaired by James Wilson, was discussing matters of local interest as the events that led to war worked themselves out. In June 1914 they were pursuing the problems of lighting, water supply and footpaths. In addition there was concern over the condition of the lifebuoy box in the Recreation Ground and the need for a lock on the boathouse. The Council wrote to Chester-le-Street Rural District Council suggesting that a convenience for women should be built at the end of Fatfield Bridge. In July they discussed how the Pontop and South Shields Railway might be opened for passenger traffic and showed concern over the fact that the boathouse, lacking a lock, was being used by gamblers and unauthorized bathers. The clerk was instructed to contact the Postmaster General to ask for a public telephone to be installed at Fatfield. They gave permission for the local miners to have a mass meeting on the Rec and agreed that the newly formed 'Fatfield Amateur Swimming Club' could erect a portable building on the Rec.

Usworth

Kelly's Directory stated, 'Usworth is a parish, which includes Great and Little Usworth and a portion of Springwell in the Chester-le-Street division of the county, east division of Chester ward, Chester-le-Street petty sessional division and union, county court district of Gateshead, rural deanery of Chester-le-Street and archdeaconry and diocese of Durham.' *Kelly's* went on to point out that the area was lit by electricity and had rail links to Gateshead and Sunderland, to give details of Holy Trinity and St Michael and All Angels and to mention the Wesleyan and Primitive Methodist chapels. Principal landowners were Viscount Boyne, Lord Ravensworth, Sir Wilfred Lawson, Bart., of Cockermouth and William G. Peareth of Rugby, Warwickshire. Usworth Colliery was owned by Johnasson, Gordon and Co and there was also a colliery at Springwell, owned by John Bowes and Partners. There were several quarries in Springwell. The population of Usworth in 1911 was 7,986.

On 24 July 1914 the Durham County Hairdressers' Association met at the Criterion Hotel in Durham and agreed that prices should be standardized at 4d for a haircut and 2d for a shave. Life was hard for many people but the price of a haircut or a shave was not one of the uncertainties. On 31 July the forty-fourth Durham Miners' Gala or 'Big Meeting' went ahead as usual, with 200 lodges marching and 100,000 visitors thronging the Racecourse. According to *The Illustrated Chronicle*, 'the peaceful invasion was greatly appreciated by the tradesfolk of the town. A Rose day was held in connection with the gathering, 70,000 artificial flowers going like hot cakes on behalf of that splendid institution, the Durham Aged Miners' Homes Association.' Those on the platform included the Dean of Worcester, John Smillie, President of the Miners' Federation, James Ramsay

MacDonald M.P. and John Wilson M.P. Suffragists were in attendance and were deserving of a photograph but they did nothing to draw any comment from the paper.

Washington Coal Company employed 1,200 workers at F Pit in 1914 and 700 at Glebe Pit; both pits were managed by Mark Ford. Usworth Colliery employed over 1,600 workers. Harraton Colliery employed 786 people underground and 175 above ground in 1914 and, at North Biddick Colliery, managed by Mr R.C. Thomas, there were 819 underground and 167 aboveground workers. It is almost certain that many of these men and women and their children were among those listening to the speeches, looking at the 'spicey stalls and monkey shows', buying from the 'aad wife selling cider' or even answering the calls of 'a chap wi' a ha'penny roondaboot shouting "noo me laads for riders".' It was summer, work was hard and the chance to eat a picnic and copy those who had 'went to Blaydon Races' was not to be missed.

Meanwhile in the chancelleries, palaces and government offices of Europe significant events were coming to a head. Looking back it is possible to argue that, by the time of the Gala, events were controlling the politicians rather than being controlled by them. Archduke Franz Ferdinand and his wife Sophie, he being heir to the throne of the Dual Monarchy of Austria-Hungary, had been assassinated on 28 June 1914 by a group of Bosnian-Serb nationalists, Gavrilo Princip firing the fatal shots, and that terrorist outrage, as many believed it to be, had set in motion a series of calculations and miscalculations that would take the lives of millions [at least 380 from Washington] and ruin the lives of millions more. Germany, encircled by enemies, was keen to support her main ally, and elements of the German government pressed for action by the hardly very reluctant Austria-Hungary against Serbia. Rapid and punitive action might, they hoped, deter other Balkan nationalists. The alternative was, it was generally thought, the gradual disintegration of Austria-Hungary.

As the miners drank and their wives looked after the kids and the kids did their best to go wild and make themselves sick on the shuggy-boats, the German Kaiser, Wilhelm II, was both issuing an ultimatum to his cousin, Tsar Nicholas II of Russia, and demanding of the French what their intentions were. Within four days Europe was at war and Sir Edward Grey made his point about the lamps going out.

CHAPTER 2

War Comes

This is not the place for a detailed description of the causes of the war or a discussion of how blame should be allocated. However, Britain had a treaty, dating back to 1839 [the scrap of paper], by which she had agreed to defend Belgium against invasion. Britain was concerned about German demands for 'a place in the sun' and how that would be a threat to the Empire. Nor did Britain, in the last resort, feel able to stand back and watch a German conquest of Europe.

Jingoistically, most people in Britain believed the war would not last long, that it would be over by Christmas and that it would certainly be over once the Hun got a taste of what the hard lads of Harraton, Fatfield, Washington, Usworth, Sheffield, Manchester, Accrington, Barnsley et al could offer him. The hard lads of Essen, Hamburg and Berlin were thinking equivalent thoughts – but in German. In France the slogan was 'l'audace, l'audace, toujours l'audace'. There had been wars within living memory in which trenches, fortifications, machine guns, artillery, submarines, stalemate and an appalling loss of life had featured heavily but they had been fought by 'The Blue' and 'The Grey' in the United States and by Russia and Japan in the Far East. European generals, it could be argued, ought to have taken more notice of them. They preferred to study Napoleon rather than Grant, Sherman, Lee, Kuroki and Kuropatkin; manoeuvre and cavalry rather than mud, minié balls and Mukden. Those fondly imagining, and forecasting, a short war, were to be proved wrong.

On 7 August 1914 *The Durham Advertiser's* leader article read as follows: 'With the suddenness of a summer thunderstorm the war cloud has descended upon Europe and before the nations have had time to grasp the tremendous significance of the fact, they find themselves engaged in the most terrible conflict the world has ever known. It is hard to realize that only a week or two since the cloud was but a darkening on the horizon, little bigger than a man's hand, so swiftly has it swooped down upon an unprepared and unsuspecting world.' The author of the article could have no idea of how terrible the conflict would actually become.

In *The Chester-le-Street Chronicle* of the same date, readers were given some advice about **'YOUR DUTY'** and were informed that the government would take charge of the food supply; were warned that they should waste nothing; were told to sit tight; were admonished to **REFUSE to Pay Panic Prices for Food** [their capitals] and were instructed **'DON'T lay in Abnormal Stores and so force prices higher.'**

Most people shopped for food at the Co-op or Walter Willson's. The latter store had taken out a full page advert in *The Illustrated Chronicle* of 10 August 1914. 'We beg to give notice to our customers that much of our stock was cleared out by the extraordinary purchasing of the Public, within 2 or 3 days of the War trouble starting.' They had immediately sought extra supplies and pointed out that, 'Any higher retail price we have asked our customers to pay results from our paying very high costs ourselves to get Food Stuffs forward.' The shop had good stocks of tea, had bacon, though at a high cost, was getting butter from Ireland, was getting large supplies of jam, was starting to use their reserve supply of pickled eggs and was selling tinned goods to the public at exact advance, having had to pay increased prices.

Birtley Co-op had branches at New Washington, Wrekenton, Ouston, Washington Station and Fatfield. In October 1914 they had 4,392 members. The Birtley Co-op quarterly report of October 1914 included an advert for families who wanted photographs taken of their men in uniform; the Co-op had made an arrangement for their members with Liddle Elliott [whose son, **Liddle Bolton Elliott**, was to be killed in action in May 1918]. The report also included details of the Special Meeting of 5 September at which the Co-op gave £100 to the Prince of Wales' Relief Fund and £100 to local distress funds.

As the report stated, 'the trade has been considerably affected by the present War Crisis and we have to report lessened profits'. Sales had amounted to £47,444 in the third quarter of the year. At New

Fatfield Branch of Birtley Co-op.

Washington there were sixty two employees and thirteen horses, at Washington Station seventeen employees and four horses and at Fatfield seven employees and one horse. The Society pointed out that under the Collective Life Assurance Scheme 'War Risks' were included, so, 'members called up will have their lives Collectively assured'. For example, '4/- in the pound on average yearly purchases for the previous three years or longer' was worth up to a limit of £40. For the wife of a member, 2/- in the pound over the same timescale would bring a death benefit of up to £20. Our motto, they pointed out, was, 'Business as usual during the War Crisis', and…,

> **'We have heard a lot about French's Contemptible Little Army but**
> **Don't Forget the Army of Young Folk**
> **At Christmastide**
> **They will expect Santa Claus as usual.'**

T.W. Bell's of Usworth Station Road were suggesting in their Christmas advert in the Washington and District Local Advertiser, 'khaki scarves, hosiery and gloves for soldiers, a variety of clothes for the ladies, toys, dolls, games and handbags for the children'. W.T. Noble's offered 'Christmas Presents for men at the front' – mostly clothes but also writing cases, while James Anderson, 'The Smart Clothier', had 'Christmas Presents for Soldiers of the King' as well as 'Pretty and Patriotic Christmas Cards'. Not far along the same street Starr's had gramophones, on easy terms, and Double-Sided records from 7d to 4 shillings – 'Come and hear before you buy'.

Just in case people had forgotten, William E. Jones, shops at Washington and Washington Station, reminded them, 'The choosing of Christmas Presents is a serious undertaking. To get exactly what one would like to give to "her" or to "him". Shall it be something Useful or Ornamental? "That is the question," as Shakespeare would say. I have pleasure in offering a few suggestions, which will meet your desires, and at the same time not seriously deplete your CASH RESERVES.' He then offered watches, brooches, rings, cigarette cases, razors, cruets, warm army clothing and '**Patriotic hearthrugs for 10s. 11d'**.

William Pattison's, Pyles' and J.D.Rutherford's were offering Christmas food of various kinds and, in case of over-eating, Miller Davison's, 'The Popular Chemist' of Washington Station, had a supply of Phosphorus and Quinine Tonic, Liquid Life at only 7½d per bottle, not to mention Dr Blaud's iron pills or K.C. Tablets, their claim being efficaciousness at cleaning the kidneys.

The Chester-le-Street Co-op meeting in January 1915 included this statement, 'Many of our members and sons of members have joined HM Forces (several hundreds we should say), this means a loss of trade to the Society to a considerable extent. Notwithstanding these adverse conditions the recording of an increase is pleasing… The clash of arms still continues with unabated fury and with an increased economic pressure further pressure is inevitable individually and collectively, you feel it we feel it… but like true Britons we will shoulder it and bear the heat and burden of the day.'

Chester-le-Street was able to give the same guarantees as Birtley re, 'War Risks', for those who had life insurance. By 1916 there were 5,129 members of the Fatfield branch.

Both Co-ops obviously played a significant role in the lives of the people of Washington. In April 1915 Birtley Co-op gave, among others,

Local Relief Funds £60.16s.0d, Belgian Relief Fund £10, allowances to employees on active service £7.17s.6d, Usworth Old People's Treat £1, Washington Old People's Treat £1. Presumably the elderly at Fatfield and Harraton were eschewing their treat for the year.

Every quarter, money, the amounts varying, was paid out to a variety of charitable organizations – Newcastle, Sunderland and Durham Infirmaries, Eye Infirmaries in the same places, Dr Barnardo's, Dame Margaret's Hall, St Dunstan's, Gilsland Convalescent Home, NSPCC, Aged Miners Homes, Poor Children's Christmas Fund, Lady Lambton's Work Depots, British Ambulance Committee, the Blind Society and many others.

[During the war total sales in the five branches of the Birtley Society rose from £211,921 in 1915 to £274,340 in 1916, to £361,150 in 1917 and £390,118 in 1918. Membership rose steadily, from 4,484 in 1915, to 5,052 in 1916, to 5,800 in 1917 and to 6,174 in 1918.

The Birtley Co-op was able to report, in 1919, that Washington had seen an increase of one per cent, Washington Station twenty-seven per cent and Fatfield of twenty four per cent. War, it turned out, was good for some businesses.]

Well, there might have been a 'war crisis' or 'war trouble' but there was good news too; 'The Reverend Hall of Chester-le-Street is coming home from his holidays in America to be among his own people at this time of crisis.' Perhaps this was the same Reverend Hall, Enoch Hall, who read the lesson as peace was celebrated in the Parish Church over four hard and bloody years later. No doubt that sent a shockwave of excitement through the paper's readers and may have, indeed, struck fear into the hearts of the German troops marching into France and 'Plucky Little Belgium'; some of those plucky little Belgians were soon to be the 'Birtley Belgians'.

The President of the Northern Centre of the National Pigeon Homing Union reminded people that pigeons had been of significant value in 1870 during the Franco-Prussian War and asked all fanciers to offer their birds to the War Office. There may be a document somewhere that details how many people and pigeons responded to the call. Pigeons were indeed used to carry messages from the front lines but whether these were the prize birds of the Homing Union…

There was no mention of the outbreak of war in the Harraton Parish Council minutes until 8 September 1914, at which point the Birtley

Iron Company was reported as finding it impossible to get gas mantles and glasses from their usual, presumably foreign, sources. The Parish responded by asking if they could not get English made ones. Mr Kirkup, agent for Lambton and Hetton Collieries, agreed that the local authorities could buy electric power from the North Biddick and Nova Scotia [Harraton Pit] sub-stations, at a cost of 2d per unit, the agreement to last five years. In addition, Washington Chemical Works was suggesting that, as the pits were working short time, the lamps could be extinguished at 11.00 pm. The Council refused the request but at the same meeting they made a request of the Lambton and Hetton Company that, from 12 September, the lamps should be extinguished at midnight and lit from 2.30 – 5 am, when of course some men would be coming off shift and others starting.

Austin Kirkup.

Chester-le-Street Rural District Council – which encompassed the Washington villages – had a number of committees operating in 1914. The first meeting of the Washington Area Committee after war was declared discussed flooding at the Cross Keys public house and, in October 1914, matters of concern included Usworth Colliery pond and Oxclose scavenging tip. In May 1915 the same topics were still exercising minds and demanding investigation. There was also discussion of the behaviour of some of the scavengers; during the winter they had been throwing ash-pit refuse on to the streets to prevent horses slipping. This was not universally popular so it was agreed to grit some of the roads. [Scavenging, and the lack of willing or reliable men to do it, was a bugbear for all councils throughout the war.] Another issue was 'offensive liquor' oozing from the Chemical Works on to the road to Washington Staithes.

Meanwhile, the Highways Committee was discussing the building of a footbridge at Cox Green. At the August 1914 meeting, figures for the year's asphalting of footpaths were given; 200 yards in Harraton, 200 yards at Usworth and 350 yards in Washington. Councillor W Bottoms, four of whose sons would join up, was one of those on the

Committee. In May 1915 the Committee noted that nine and a quarter miles of roads in the area were used by motor omnibuses and needed strengthening.

The first mention of war in the Barmston Parish minutes was in September 1914. Washington Chemicals had suggested reducing the lighting in the area – which the council rejected, whilst they had had a letter from the Board of Agriculture with leaflets suggesting that gardens and allotments ought to be cultivated. A letter from Chester-le-Street Relief Fund suggested that Barmston should set up a sub-committee for relief. Presumably in the belief that it was going to be 'over by Christmas', the minutes note, 'After discussing the project and the prospect being that there would be very little, if any, distress in the parish arising from the war, it was resolved to join with Washington Parish.' One of the councillors was Charles Wiseman, who died late in 1914. His son, **Thomas**, would be killed near Armentières on New Year's Eve 1915.

Washington Parish Council took a more active approach to the outbreak of war. At their September meeting they arranged for Reverend Holmes to address a public meeting at the Village Green on 14 August, while Mark Ford, manager of both Glebe and F Pits, would speak at Brady Square. Whether the intention was to promote recruiting or calm people's fears was not made clear.

DON'T BE A LAMBTON WORM!

Lord Lambton struck a martial note at the Chester-le-Street Co-operative Hall when he pointed out that the three sons of his twin brother were in the army [one of them, the Honourable Francis Lambton, was killed on 31 October 1914] and so were the husbands of his two daughters. He advised young women, when being courted, to say, 'What are you going to do? Are you going to fight? If you are not you are not good enough for me.' No doubt the young ladies took him at his word. Perhaps they described those lads who were not eager to serve as 'Lambton worms'? In addition to offering advice to courting girls, the noble Lord was making sacrifices; he announced that there was to be no shooting on his estate since he was handing it over for the good of the nation, for the benefit of the sick and the wounded. He was also doing his bit at recruiting stations, visiting Shiney Row, among others, on 29 August. In November he attended the Sunderland Empire for a joint recruiting and family relief event. Later in the month he appeared at the same kind of function at the Theatre Royal, Newcastle and on the 26th he attended a patriotic concert at the Alexandra Theatre, Washington, an event that was intended to raise money for Belgian refugees as well as local families. In December he appeared at the Victoria Hall, Sunderland and chose to defend some of his earlier remarks, in which he had said that he might wish a German shell to drop on Roker Park if that was the only way of waking up the young men of Sunderland, not as many of whom as he would have liked had joined up.

Professional football had continued [even though Lord Hawke had announced that there would be no County Championship cricket in the summer of 1915] and there was discussion in the papers about whether this was appropriate. Mr Spedding of the Durham Football Association had written to the Earl, stating that 3,520 recruits, players and officials of the 380 clubs affiliated to the Durham FA had enlisted. Lord Durham was wrong, noted Mr Spedding, to say that was ten per cent of the possible total since it was actually fifty per cent of Durham FA club members, an average of nine per club.

There were lots of men for whom Lord Lambton's entreaties were unnecessary. Mr Goodley, headmaster of Fatfield Council School, first mentioned the war in the Log Book on 14 September 1914, 'Mr Watson was absent today to enlist in the army'. On 24 September, '**Mr Metcalfe** was absent this morning having gone to enlist'. Another teacher, **James Francis Gordon Ashworth**, enlisted in September 1915 and W.B. Toyer and Mr Stables were others from his staff who served.

Lt James Francis Gordon Ashworth. (Ulverston High School)

On the day of **Mr Metcalfe's** enlistment, the Log recorded, 'The girls are beginning to knit stockings and make garments for the soldiers in the war. Lady Lambton has kindly sent £2 to buy materials.'

Meanwhile, the common phrase of the day among the pitmen was, apparently, 'Wad thou gan ti the front if they wanted thou?' – to which the only possible answer for these hard lads was, 'Why aye,' – in which case they'd have satisfied the young ladies, as well as Lord Lambton.

Another [apochryphal?] story – 'The paper says that the Kayzer is gannin to impose Jarmin kultur on aal the people in the world. Worrisit, this kultur?'

'Wey, a kind of Jarmin polony myed oot of deed horses.'

'By gox, that settles it, aa'm gannin te enlist, we'll hae nae kultur hya.'

Just in case the bellicose enthusiasm of patriotic Washington pitmen and the exhortations of Lord Lambton were insufficient, there were heroes adding to the mood of national mobilization. On 4 September readers of *The Chester-le-Street Chronicle* were able to read the letter from Mr J.W.H.T. Douglas, Mr F.R. Foster, Reverend F.H. Gillingham, Mr W.G. Grace, Lord Harris, Hayward T., Hirst G.H., Hobbs J.B., Mr G.L. Jessop, Rhodes W., Mr R.H. Spooner, Mr P.F. Warner and Woolley F.E., who were appealing on behalf of the Prince of Wales' Fund for cases of misery and hardship. These were thirteen of the greatest English cricketers who ever lived. Another great cricketer was His Highness Jam Sahib of Nawanagar, Kumar Shri Ranjitsinhji and he was made an Honorary Colonel, for recruiting purposes, in December 1914. Some of those men were gentlemen, as noted by 'Mr', 'Lord,' or 'Reverend'; and some of them were players, mere professionals indeed, who were entitled to initials – but only **after** their surnames. Of course, Mr W.G. Grace [retired since 1908] was not only the most famous player, possibly the most famous man, in England in Victorian times but also the best paid, by far. He was, of course, an amateur. An appreciation of Latin declensions, Greek verses and the fag system probably made the whole thing easier to understand. They were, indeed, 'class' players.

In December 1914 it was reported in *The Illustrated Chronicle* that thirteen Test Match cricketers, not content with offering their names to recruiting drives, had joined the colours, as had many other county players. One of the former was the oddly named Major Booth, who had joined the Leeds Pals and whose grave [Lieutenant Major Booth] is in Serre Road No. 1 Cemetery. Not to be outdone, a Footballers' Battalion was established and one who enlisted was **William Jonas** of Clapton Orient, whose wife lived in Shafto Terrace, Washington. (See page 74)

Also in December, a group that included some officials from North Biddick Colliery made a 'fine effort', at Penshaw, to raise money for clothing for soldiers. With songs and recitations, Messrs Fennell, J.

Kelly, W. Rogerson, R.A. Duncan, T. Sanderson, J.R. Jopling, G. Liddle, W. and E. McCarton, R.C. Thomas, Reverend Holmes, Mrs Long and Miss Kelly gave everyone who attended a splendid evening and they had their picture printed in *The Illustrated Chronicle*. Mr Kelly's son, **Michael**, was to be killed in January 1917 and is commemorated on the Thiepval Memorial.

At the Alexandra and Glebe, in Washington, people could watch, *The Adventures of Kathleen*, *Mabel's Nerve* or *The Bowery Boys*, – all made by Keystone Films and at prices of 2d, 3d or 4d. Kathleen's Adventures, however exciting, were not going to match those of Washington's bravest and best who, when leaving by train, would have had 'Land of Hope and Glory', 'Rule Britannia' and the 'National Anthem' ringing in their ears.

Patriotic fervour and suspicion of 'the enemy within' resulted in a number of incidents of sentries shooting people who had not replied properly or had been in boats and failed to hear a challenge. Pork butchers, whose numbers included several with German names, had a hard time as their shops were damaged by crowds. In Washington, John Fredrick Konig was a pork butcher at Speculation Place, his assistant another German, Ernest Russ. It is not known what happened to these men but no one by either name is recorded in the death registers, so it may be that they returned to Germany or changed their names. Hermann Hochstein, a German-born colliery boiler-maker, who lived and worked in Washington in 1911, died in Kettering in 1918. Perhaps he had been forced to move away. In Sunderland, the German ex-Consul, Nicholaus Emil Herman Adolph Ahlers, was arrested for high treason, found guilty and sentenced to death. He had apparently been unaware of the actual declaration of war when he advised some Germans to leave the country and his ignorance of these facts was, at his appeal, used to exonerate him. He did, however, have to move from Sunderland because of the harassment of his family and home. He moved to Surbiton and changed his name to Anderson but, according to *The Illustrated Chronicle*, was interned in July 1915.

Local newspapers reported the details of the Grace Hume case. This blameless nurse from Huddersfield had a sister who had, in keeping with the excited tenor of the times, written to the newspapers about the rape, mutilation and murder of the aforementioned Grace. Grace had not however, been anywhere further south than Huddersfield and, while there may have been pork butchers of German extraction in that town, there were neither Uhlans nor Prussians. In short, Grace was fine. When her sister was tried in Edinburgh in December 1914, she was found guilty of a 'Bogus Atrocity' story but treated, to everyone's satisfaction, with leniency and, having spent three months in jail already, was released to a cheering crowd. After all, if the Germans had not raped, mutilated and murdered Grace then they had, as their own documents showed, done those things to many innocent Belgians.

The reasons why men joined up would have been many and varied. Life down the pit was undoubtedly hard and dangerous – *The Durham Advertiser* noted in October 1915 that there had been forty six fatalities in that year so far in County Durham's pits, caused by roof falls as a result of either a shortage of timber or a lack of proper inspection – and the prospect of some excitement in a foreign land was one that seems to have appealed to many.

What, you may be wondering, of 'shirkers or weary Willies'? Well, it was reported that Chester-le-Street Union Relief Committee would be offering them no help. The Union was responsible for administering assistance to those at the bottom of the social pile, a pile below which there were only weary willies and shirkers, presumably. The Liberal government in the pre-war period had introduced Old Age Pensions for those over seventy and Sickness and Unemployment Insurance for workmen but 'shirkers and weary Willies' were obviously going to get no assistance from any of these schemes. No sir.

It did not take long before local firms began to use the war in their advertising. In October 1914 Robert Sinclair of Grainger Street, Newcastle, was offering to send half a pound of tobacco, 100 cigarettes and a pipe to men serving abroad for the duty-free price of two shillings. By the end of 1915 the same firm was reminding readers of *The Illustrated Chronicle* that the last posting day for 'Christmas smokes for Tommy and Jack at the Dardanelles' was 16 November. A Newcastle Insurance Broker was advertising insurance against Zeppelin attacks and the clothing firm, Stewart's, was advertising various clothes made of the same khaki as the government contracts were using. For 42s, khaki suits were available, great coats were 57/6d, trousers 15/6d and service jackets 28/6d. Very few of the Washington volunteers, no doubt, were obliged to wait for government contracts to be fulfilled since many of these items were over a week's wages for a miner.

And, once the terrible realities of war began to sink in and the casualty lists began to appear, there were other marketing opportunities:

'THE SOLDIER'S FRIEND
A Friend in Need is a Friend Indeed
SOLDIERS FRIENDS AND RELATIONS
WE SELL
MASON'S BULLET-PROOF AND SHRAPNEL-PROOF
LIFE-SAVER.
SOLDIERS DON'T BE KILLED
WEAR MASON'S LIFE SAVER
PROTECTS VITAL PARTS
PRICES ONLY 5/- EACH (Postage 4d Extra)
ALL-BRITISH BULLET-PROOF LIFE SAVER COMPANY
CROSS STREET, WESTGATE ROAD, NEWCASTLE.'

If only it had been so simple. The advert appeared in *The Illustrated Chronicle* early in the war but was not repeated.

On Friday, 11 September 1914, Robert Heslop of Felling printed what he called the 'First Edition of Washington and District Volunteer Record', at a cost of 1d, all proceeds to go to local relief funds. The heading summed up the situation, 'Their King and Country Need Them!' 'They have Answered THE CALL.' The four pages consisted, of a list of 392 men who had joined up by 4 pm, 8 September. The list was divided into 265 names for 'Lord Kitchener's New Army', seventy-nine names of men 'Serving His Majesty (but particulars of service not known; all employed by Usworth Colliery)', twenty eight names of, 'Reservists who have joined the colours', fifteen Territorials, and five men who had, 'Officially signified their willingness to serve, to be called up when required'. The latter group may have all been teachers, certainly four of them had school names attached. There followed a request for other men to sign up and for those wishing or able to join the Ambulance Service. The information had been supplied by local employers of labour and by the sergeant in charge of the Recruiting Station at the National Schools, Washington. Of the 102 Harraton men killed in the war, at least thirty seven had enlisted at Shiney Row. No copies of later editions of the *Advertiser* have been found.

Half a column was then devoted to listing the members of the five, 'Area Relief Committees', whose task was to respond to requests from those in 'necessitous circumstances' in order to 'relieve distress'. [And distress there was; the Housing Committee noted in February 1915, about rent arrears in Washington and Usworth, that 'where tenants have been seriously affected by the shortage of work or the enlistment of the wage earners', then rent collectors should ascertain details and report back to the committee.]

Committee members included a number of clergymen, councillors, wives of Justices of the Peace and Head Teachers from local schools – the great and the good of Washington and Usworth. In Harraton, similar arrangements were made and, in September 1914, the Fatfield Mothers' Union sent to the Northumberland Fusiliers the following: two dozen triangular bandages, six towels, one dozen pairs of pillow slips, six bed-jackets, six shirts, eleven pairs of socks, six flannelette nightshirts, five pairs of stockings. It was the start of much knitting, repairing and bandage rolling and the articles no doubt made camp-life more bearable for a few, but there was a great deal more to be done and supplying a hugely increased army was going to be beyond even the rapid knitters of the Mothers' Union.

Usworth and Springwell Red Cross Guild were raising money from raffles and donations and they had managed to send, 'every man at the Front, either actively fighting or helping in Red Cross Work, a parcel consisting of a shirt, Cardigan jacket, body belt, socks, mitts, muffler, helmet, Xmas pudding, Xmas cake, cigarettes, chocolates and Xmas card'.

By October 1914 the Soldiers and Sailors Families Association was in operation and Miss Reeman, of the Vicarage, had become the Fatfield representative on Lady Durham's working parties.

Of course, even while men were being exhorted to do their patriotic and manly duty others were already being killed in France.

CHAPTER 3

First Casualties

Michael Grafton was Washington's first casualty. He was killed in action on 21 September 1914, having gone to France as recently as 8 September. He had been listed in the Washington and District Volunteer Record, a reservist who had rejoined the colours.

The 1911 Census listed **Michael** as, 'Overseas Military'. He was then serving in the 1st Battalion Durham Light Infantry at Nasirabad-Rajputana and his age was given as twenty three. Michael's service record states that he enlisted on 6 November 1906 at the age of eighteen years and three months. The record of his medical examinations outlines some of the places in which he served – Newcastle, Cork, Lucknow in October 1908, Nasirabad in February 1909 and Peshawar in April 1912. He seems to have been fairly healthy despite a week in hospital in Noushera in August 1912, suffering from dyspepsia, and another spell while in Peshawar, the reason indecipherable.

A reading of his disciplinary record suggests that he kept tropical diseases away by liberal ingestion of strong alcohol. Drunkenness was a problem for **Michael** and his disciplinary record was littered with instances of it – in barracks, in camp, while he should have been practising musketry, etc. He often exacerbated his problems with obscenities and threats and regularly refused orders and tasks. On one occasion he broke out of incarceration. In 1908 he was found in possession of a 26lb cheese from the Garrison Coffee Bar and was fined for doing 3s worth of [unspecified – you are allowed to wonder] damage to the cheese. He suffered confinement to barracks, fines and imprisonment but it seems to have made little difference. The word 'incorrigible' seems apt.

Incorrigible or not, **Michael** found himself at the sharp end of the war in 1914 and was killed in September. The form sent, in August 1915, by the army to the next of kin, went to Emma Mooney, a cousin, of 20 Albert Terrace, Usworth. She stated that his father was Stephen Fitzpatrick of Springwell, that his mother was unknown but that he had two half-blood sisters, Phoebe and Ellen, addresses unknown.

Michael's record includes a letter from Stephen Fitzpatrick of 1 Clarence Terrace, Springwell, dated May 1920, that reads:

'Dear Sir, I received my son's memorial card witch (sic) I am very greatly pleased and thankful for. This is the first word I have had from the War Office about anything concerning my dear son.

I saw in the papers he was killed on 8th October 1914. I have being [sic] waiting a few months till things got sorted out a bit.

I am married again and … a wife …and little family but I am writing to say I have not worked for 5 years unable through being ruptured and I am up in years makes things worse.

I am yours faithfully
Stephen Fitzpatrick

1st Durhams was his Battalion but we don't know what Durhams he was in when lost.'

The 2nd Durhams had marched over 40 kilometres in the days prior to a German attack that took place near Troyon on 20 September. According to the War Diary, 'the Battalion on the right gave way, reported to be caused by a white flag incident', and forced a withdrawal. Casualties for 20 September were noted in the Battalion War Diary as Major Mander, Captain Hare and thirty six other ranks killed. Though **Michael**'s death is listed as 21 September it is possible that he was one of the casualties from 20 September since the War Diary lists no casualties for 21 September. [Only rarely do war diaries include the names of Other Ranks killed – officers were normally named.]

Mrs Mooney received **Michael**'s 1914 Star in September 1919 and his War and Victory medals in 1920. However, his father received the scroll and plaque. **Michael** is commemorated on Usworth Memorial and on the memorial by the River Marne at La Ferté-sous-Jouarre.

John T. Lennox was born in St Andrew's, Northumberland. He served as Private 3502, Coldstream Guards, and was killed, according to his Medal Roll, 'on or since 22 December 1914'. The Washington and District Volunteer Record had listed **John Lennox** of Usworth Station Road, a reservist who had joined the colours. He is commemorated on Le Touret Memorial and Washington Memorial. He was awarded the 1914 Star and the War and Victory medals.

In 1901 **John T. Lennox** was living at Chelsea Barracks, a soldier in the Coldstream Guards. The 1911 Census lists **John Lenox** [sic] living as a boarder with the family of Henry Jenkins at 2 New Rows, Usworth. **John** was a stoneman. The mis-spelling may be due to the fact that the census form had been filled in by Mr Jenkins, apparently uncertain of his boarder's exact name. *The Illustrated Chronicle* of 8 February 1916 reported the death of **J.T. Lennox** of Washington but gave no further details. The Commonwealth War Graves Commission lists no **J.T. Lennox** killed in 1916, so perhaps the lateness of the information was as a result of his family coming to terms with his loss or even, perhaps, that he had no surviving family.

The War Diary of 1st Coldstreams records that on 20 December 1914 they were ordered to march at 5 pm and reached Béthune, 20 miles away, at midnight. The Germans had attacked the Indian Corps on 20 December, the latter losing nineteen officers and 815 other ranks as prisoners. The Guards were sent to stabilize the situation and did so, though the Guards Division lost over 1,800 men, some of them to frostbite and exposure as they lay out without cover for 2/3 days in flooded trenches. On 21 December the Guards Division attacked at Givenchy and on the 22nd they renewed/continued their attack, three companies being used to attack German trenches on the line of the Givenchy to Chapelle St Roche road. The Coldstreams took their main objective but were then bombed out and retired, having lost fifty per cent of their strength. Specifically, on 21st–22nd, they had lost one officer killed, one officer died of wounds, ten other ranks killed, 128 other ranks wounded and fifty seven other ranks missing.

The Roll of Honour drawn up for Washington and Barmston Parishes included **John Lennox** and gave his address as 8 Ellen Terrace. He is also listed on the Memorial to the men of F Pit, Washington, that was unveiled in 1921 by J. Olds, Lodge Treasurer.

On 2 April it was reported, 'At the Miners Hall Washington, on

Saturday night, a large audience assembled at the unveiling of a memorial tablet in memory of the men of the F Pit Lodge Durham Miners' Association who died in the war. Mr John Cullen, president of the lodge, presided. At the outbreak of the war there were 1,084 men and boys employed at the colliery, of whom 436 joined the colours, and out of this number sixty-four gave their lives.

The memorial tablet, which is made of oak, standing on a stone base, is ten feet nine inches in height and six feet three inches in width. On the centre panel are inscribed in gold the names of the sixty-four men who made the supreme sacrifice for King and Country. The tablet, which is placed inside the hall, was erected by the Co-operative Wholesale Society Pelaw works, and cost about £200.'

The February-March edition of the Washington Holy Trinity Church magazine included a list of six members of the choir and fifty-three others for whom the congregation had been asked to pray. **John Lennox** was one of those not in the choir.

John Dunn(e), of the Royal Irish Regiment, whose death was announced in January 1915, was the first Harraton man to be killed abroad. **Private Dunn(e)** was described as 'formerly a miner at Fatfield'. The Commonwealth War Graves Commission states that he was originally from Dungannon and it may be that he had returned there before the war. He was killed on 19 October 1914 and his name appears both on the Le Touret Memorial and Harraton Memorial.

George Crichton died in February 1915. Little is known about **George**'s service but it appears that he died without having been abroad. He has no Service Record, no Medal Roll entry and no Pension Record. His name appears on the Harraton Memorial [being one of those added after the unveiling, which may suggest he was not long in the village or did not have any relations to make sure his name was on the original list]. *St George's Gazette*, the monthly magazine for the Northumberland Fusiliers, noted in February that the men had been supplied with khaki greatcoats, which made them 'more soldierly'. It stated that Tring, 'has a lamentable lack of attractions in the shape of amusement', so the soldiers had organized a couple of concerts and had played the Royal Field Artillery at Berkhamstead and won 4-2, 'tea being kindly provided by the local YMCA. Nothing definite has been heard re our removal to hutments so, as before, we remain in the billets of the householders of Tring.' There had been some changes in the location of a couple of companies and 'there were sad partings and the interruptions of many pleasant "walking outs" but the soldier soon acclimatizes himself to change, and we hear of dances and strolls in these new surroundings'.

The local [Tring] paper was quoted in *St George's Gazette,* 'The soldiers in Tring are having a strenuous time. Route marches, night attacks, and other field exercises are carried on side by side with courses of musketry instruction. Platoons are told off daily for fatigue duty and are employed digging trenches…

'Musketry courses and the building of curious looking bridges are carried out in a masterly way in spite of the distractions offered by the emus which Lord Rothschild has kindly placed at our disposal together with Tring Park. We have also to set on record our gratitude to his children who have made a most generous gift of tobacco and cigarettes to the men.

'On 11th we stimulated ourselves by putting on our khaki uniforms for a march-past and inspection by the Brigadier.' **George Crichton** would not have been part of that because *St George's* ended the notes on 13 Battalion with, 'It is with sincere regret that we too have to close these notes by recording the death of **Private Crichton** of D Company'. His death occurred, no reason was given, on 10 February and he was buried in Tring Cemetery.

CHAPTER 4

Well We Don't Want to Lose You ... But We'll be Proud of You if You Go

Those who enlisted were generally described as 'Local Heroes'. By 23 October 1914 *The Chester-le-Street Chronicle* had listed twenty eight men from Harraton who had joined, probably at Shiney Row or perhaps in Newcastle, what the paper described as 'Kitchener's Army' – mostly the Tyneside Irish, the Tyneside Scottish or the Commercials.

The bombardment of Hartlepool in December 1914 was, naturally, used as an example of the beastliness of The Hun and there were stories of the death, destruction and subsequent burials; full page adverts appeared encouraging men to join up in order to exact revenge for the 'East Coast Outrage'.

Of course, while every individual man who volunteered was a 'Local Hero' the local press recognized that patriotic feeling could be fostered by featuring whole families of local heroes. As early as May 1915 *The Chester-le-Street Chronicle* announced that they were very happy to print photos of the local heroes, that the printing was free and that it came with a guarantee that all photos would be returned safely. Later, as casualty lists grew, the heading, 'Local Hero' began to mean those who had been killed or died. Later in the war *The Chester-le-Street Chronicle* felt obliged to charge 2/6d for the printing of photos.

'Mr John Neal of Washington,' it was reported in January 1915, 'has given almost his whole family to the Army'; photographs of his four sons, a nephew and two sons-in-law were featured. All appear to have survived the war. According to the same source, on 13 February 1915, Councillor W. Bottoms of Usworth Colliery had four sons and a son-in-law with the colours; again, all survived. James Button's four soldier sons were pictured on 9 March 1915 – all survived the war.

In May 1915 it was reported that Thomas Bloomfield, of 1 Harraton Colliery, had joined the Durham Fortress Engineers. In August 1915 W. Bloomfield of Harraton Colliery joined the Tyneside Scottish and that made a total of four brothers serving, the other two being Joseph (Royal Army Medical Corps) and Lancelot (Royal Garrison Artillery). Their father was a master shifter at Harraton Colliery and a special constable.

Another featured family of local heroes were the Lavertys. On 23 July 1915 the '5 Laverty brothers in service' were shown. They were Jack, Edward and Thomas in the Durham Light Infantry, Daniel in the Royal Navy and **Joe,** killed in 1917, in the Royal Garrison Artillery.

And when a connected group of men enlisted that was also a cause for publicity – thus in May 1915 *The Illustrated Chronicle* reported, 'The Washington Station United Methodist Church Brotherhood has responded nobly to the country's call. Out of a membership of fifty-two, the number that responded was forty-one. Only two failed to pass the army medical examiner and thirty-five out of the thirty-nine accepted are single men. One has since met his death [**John Edward Green,** born in Penshaw, went to France on 19 April 1915, was killed in action a mere eight days later and is buried in Vlamertinghe Cemetery] on the battlefield, and at present about thirteen are on the various battlefields in France, Belgium and the Dardanelles. The others are in training with the regiments they are attached to.'

Joseph Sproul, Ernest Seed, Charles Ball, Fred Wilson, John Reay Pittilla, Benjamin White, Thomas Paxton, John Smith, Thomas Allen and **Robert Bateman** were others of the Methodist Brotherhood who would not be coming home.

Not to be outdone, Washington Holy Trinity Church sent in to *The Illustrated Chronicle* a composite photograph of one hundred members of the church and choir who had enlisted. The Vicar, Reverend Lomax, a chaplain in 8 DLI, was at the centre. The February–March 1915 edition of the Holy Trinity magazine listed six members of the choir

Mawson family. (Family)

and fifty-three others for whom church-goers were praying. Now there were over a hundred. At least seventeen of the fifty-nine mentioned in the parish magazine were to be killed.

Of course it was not only patriotism that led men to join. The Mawson family story is that **George William** and a friend had 'gone on the hoy' to Newcastle and, having run out of money, decided to join up there. The friend survived. The story is told that **Private Mawson**'s children were always well fed but never knew in which

George W Mawson. (Family)

house they would get their dinner, the family being very poor and neighbours taking pity on the children. **George** was killed in action on 22 September 1916 and buried at Bécourt Military Cemetery, close to Albert.

It appears that Lord Kitchener had some understanding of the soldierly temperament. The 1st Battalion Tyneside Irish attended church services at St Nicholas' Cathedral, St Mary's Roman Catholic

Mawson's original grave. (Family)

Cathedral and various nonconformist churches in Newcastle on 15 February 1915, at which they were advised, in the words of the owner of the most famous finger ever featured on a poster, to avoid the two dangers to soldiers, 'wine and women'. No doubt the men had their own views but who could risk ignoring the words of the face on the ubiquitous posters? Probably quite a lot of them could, given a fair chance.

On 4 June 1915 *The Durham Advertiser* carried an advert for the Tyneside Irish Brigade. 'More Recruits Wanted for this Popular Brigade. Apply JM Lynch, North Road, Durham.' The popularity of the Brigade no doubt had something to do with the high numbers of Irish immigrants who had settled in the North East during the second half of the nineteenth century. When recruiting posters were first issued for the Tyneside Irish, in October 1914, the wording had included the following, 'Those who are inspired by that love of freedom dominant in the Irish race, and which is threatened by the German lust of power, should enrol themselves now in the Tyneside Irish Battalion and preserve for themselves and their children that glorious liberty so dear to the heart of every Irishman.' Lord Kitchener, Sir John French, Lord Roberts and General Smith-Dorrien were described as Irish and 'the greatest fighting men of our time'. Whether these soaring phrases and sentiments applied to those Irishmen whose love of freedom was mainly expressed in a desire to gain independence from Britain, was not made clear.

Once the fighting Irish had seen action another recruiting lever became available. The Victoria Cross won at Cuinchy by Sergeant Michael O'Leary of the Irish Guards showed just what 'Paddies' could do (i.e. take two German machine gun posts and kill or wound ten Germans) and he was feted, received his VC from the King, had a short play written about him by George Bernard Shaw, toured the country and starred in recruiting posters. 'Don't Stand and Cheer, But Come and Join Me,' was his call. Plenty from the North East did just that.

Another spur to recruitment was the Zeppelin threat. Joseph Cowen of Stella Hall, Blaydon, offered £500 to the first airmen to shoot down a Zeppelin.

Regular listings of those men who had joined the Tyneside Irish, the Tyneside Scots, the Commercials and the Royal Inniskilling Fusiliers appeared. It was not exactly a race but there was a sense of competition and, by 13 January 1915, the Tyneside Scots were able to claim 'victory' in as much as they had signed up four full battalions of men with depot companies – a total of 5,400 men. Later in the year, as casualty lists lengthened and volunteering diminished, Lord Derby's

Scheme was introduced and the Tyneside Scots produced a poster which invited men to join as follows:

'TYNESIDE SCOTTISH BRIGADE
Harder than Hammers
LORD DERBY'S CAMPAIGN
Men now enlisting under the campaign of Lord Derby are cordially invited to select the Reserve Battalion of the above Brigade which comprises the pick of Tyneside Fighting Men now trained and ready to depart Overseas.

Chief Recruiting Office: 9 GRAINGER STREET WEST, NEWCASTLE UPON TYNE. Open all day until 8.30 each night or enlistment can be insured [sic] at any Recruiting Office.

God Save The King.'

In July 1915 local newspapers carried the news that Lord Kitchener was calling for 300,000 more men. In order to enhance the patriotic spirit, the London Caledonian Pipe Band attended a series of open-air meetings at which recruits to the Durham Light Infantry could enlist but, 'recruits will be accepted for any other Regiment they desire to join'. On Wednesday, 28 July, the band was due at Springwell at 3.30 pm, Great Usworth at 4.30, Washington at 5.30, Washington Station at 6.30 and Fatfield at 7.30, presumably marching between the venues. The newspaper entry ended with **'MEN OF THE CHESTER-LE-STREET DIVISION: YOUR COUNTRY NEEDS YOU: GOD SAVE THE KING.'**

In October 1915 another appeal **'TO MY PEOPLE'** was issued in the King's name. He wrote of an, 'organized enemy who has transgressed the Laws of Nations and changed the ordinance that binds civilized Europe together'. He rejoiced in the Empire's effort and its great sacrifices, 'in order that another may not inherit the free Empire which their ancestors and mine have built,' and ended by stating that responding to his appeal, 'will be giving your support to our brothers, who, for long months, have nobly upheld Britain's past traditions, and the glory of her arms'.

CHAPTER 5

1915 ... Summary: Bother at the Bridge, Tribunals, Gallipoli, Loos

The general hope and expectation that the war would be over by Christmas 1914 was already seen to be over-optimistic as 1915 dawned. The country was gearing up for a long war, getting used to casualty lists in the newspapers [at least forty-nine Washington men were killed in 1915] and realizing that women would have an important role to play. On the Western Front the early movement had ground to a halt and a front was established from the Channel to the Swiss border. During the year there were battles at Neuve Chapelle and Loos, the Germans used poison gas at Ypres, British, French and Anzac troops fought at Gallipoli, German submarine warfare intensified, Sir Douglas Haig became Commander in Chief of the British armies and Zeppelins bombed Britain. Perhaps one of their targets was Fatfield Bridge, a significant, and therefore guarded, crossing of the Wear.

Bother at the Bridge
Fatfield Bridge (*The Chester-le-Street Chronicle* called it Biddick Bridge) had been placed under military guard and on 10 July 1915 there was an incident concerning the bridge, the soldiers guarding it and some of 'the lads', specifically George William Ashford and Henry Young. Young and Ashford were prosecuted under the Defence of the

Fatfield Bridge.

Realm Act (DORA), the charges against them being that they 'interfered with a sentry'.

Private G. Hebburn of the Royal Garrison Artillery was on guard at the northern end of the bridge when, at 21.05 hours, the miscreants, as they were very soon to become, approached. As he had been trained to do, Hebburn challenged them, probably something along the lines of, 'Halt who goes there?' Events began to go downhill from that point. Did Ashford and Young know Hebburn, had they drunk strong ale with him in the Ferryboat Inn or even ginger beer in Flannigan's Temperance Inn? Yes, a temperance pub. They were unused to being challenged (at least by soldiers) as they made their way home, probably slightly tipsy, perhaps roaring drunk, perhaps even stone cold sober. In a way it was inevitable that they would ignore the first challenge. However, when two further challenges by the dutiful Private Hebburn were also ignored, he proceeded to the next level of alert and blew his whistle to summon the commander of the guard. Hebburn could, by military law, have shot Ashford and Young for ignoring three challenges (a pretty severe version of 'three strikes and you're out' but, hey, there was a war on) and so, presumably, could Lance Corporal Simpson, commander of the guard. Instead, Simpson contented himself with asking Ashford what he was doing – or, perhaps, rough military words to that effect. Ashford, perhaps emboldened by drink, and certainly aware of the international situation, responded, 'You might be a b... ... German.' There might be death, dysentery and destruction at Gallipoli and there was heavy fighting all around Ypres but *The Chester-le-Street Chronicle* was d...ed if it was going to print b.. language. When Lance Corporal Simpson repeated his question, Ashford inquired, presumably with some vim and perhaps with some expletives added, 'What has it to do with you?'

Given the gravity of the situation and the possible threat to good order, an officer needed to become involved but, very unfortunately under the circumstances, and bearing in mind Ashford's earlier stated concerns about the possible presence of the enemy disguised as British troops, it was, at best unfortunate, at worst a red rag to a bull, that the officer in question was called Lieutenant Liebricht. It does not require much imagination to guess how things went from that point.

'Whe are ye, bonny lad, and has tha started shavin yet? Stannin aboot with ya bluddy swagger stick, an' ya shiny boots an' askin'stupid bloody questions.'

'Lt Liebricht, and yes, I shave.'

'Come again, marra? Did ye just say Lieutenant Liebricht? Geordie, did that fella really just say Lieutenant Leeeebb – richt? What kind of name is Leeeeee - bricht, then, when it's at hyem? Sounds like a bloody Jarmin name to me. Aa telt thee, Geordie, the buggers have invaded aalriddy. Run, bonny lad, afore the bugger shoots us! Hey, missus, lock up ya bairns, the Jarmins hev invaded!!'

The upshot of the matter was that Ashford and Young admitted to the magistrates that they had been drunk and were sentenced to a month in prison. There is a faded photograph of a Sergeant Liebricht, serving in India, pre-war, in Durham County Record Office. He had obviously been promoted when the war began.

She could bite, could Dora.

Tribunals

Not everyone showed the same enthusiasm for war, adventure, or getting away from the pit as those men who flocked to join in the early days of the war. That led to the government passing the Conscription Act in January 1916 and to the establishment of local tribunals to rule on the cases of those who sought exemption on grounds such as conscience, disability, family and business. [All tribunal papers were destroyed in 1921 except some exemplars held in the National Archives.]

Nathan Marshall, killed on the Somme in August 1916, served in the Non Combatant Corps as a stretcher bearer; we can assume that, like Sydney Estell, aged eighteen, of Birtley, **Nathan** had applied for absolute exemption on conscientious grounds. In his statement of claim, as quoted in *The Chester-le-Street Chronicle,* Estell said, 'My reasons are moral and religious. The Divine law says, "Thou shalt not kill" and I believe that means me to obey. Therefore I have the strongest possible objection to take part in the destruction or injury of human life in any circumstances whatever. I feel whatever the consequences I must obey the views of conscience.'

On being called before the Military Tribunal, whose task was to assess the cases of those seeking exemption, he began, without waiting to be asked, to state his case, and said, 'My friends I wish to state my case before you. I claim the protection of the law under the Military Service Act and I can demand from this Tribunal...'

At that point he was interrupted by the Chairman and asked a series of very typical questions. Some are shown below with Sydney's answers.

'Mr Sharp: Did you ever have a fight? – Not to my knowledge.

Mr James Hall: If someone gave you a blow on the cheek would you turn the other one? – Yes.

Mr James Wilson: How long have you been a Primitive Methodist? – Since I was 14.

Mr Wilson: What are you working at in the pits? – As a banksman at the Bewicke Main D Pit under the Birtley Iron and Coal Company. I expect my employers will appeal for me but I am appealing as a conscientious objector on my own part.

Mr Pearce: You do not believe in the Good Samaritan? – I might but not under the military oath.

Mr Sharp: If the Germans came and dropped bombs and people were wounded would you do nothing to assist them? – No.

Mr Hall: Have you a mother? – Yes.

Mr Hall: a sister? – No.

Mr Hall: Suppose the Germans came and outraged your mother, would you take your stand and defend her? – I might defend her but I would not kill, even if it was at the price of my mother's life.'

Sydney was recommended for non-combatant service. His Military Service Record states that he served as Private 970 in Number 2 Northern Company of the Non Combatant Corps from May 1916. Sidney became part of the BEF in France on 28 May but no further information is given about his activities, or lack of them, while in France, nor how long he was there. His enrolment form mentions Richmond, where some of the conscientious objectors were held under extremely rigorous conditions but, again, no information is given.

A letter from someone who supported the conscientious objectors was printed in *The Chester-le-Street Chronicle* in March 1916. 'Mr Sharp says we are fighting in defence of religion but for the life of me I cannot see any difference between Mr Sharp's religion and that of the Kaiser. Both of them believe that the God is on the side of the big battalions and both believe that no one should hold or express an opinion different from his.'

Corporal Gray, DLI, not surprisingly, held a different view when referring to Mr Estell, 'I don't believe he is a Christian. Oh no, if he spoke the truth he would say "I am a coward."' He went on to quote his own selection of the scriptures and argued that, in the light of what had been done to innocent Belgians by the Germans, their air raids on Britain and the awful consequences of defeat, men should shake off the conscientious feeling and come forward to join the 'Faithfuls', the nickname of 8 DLI.

'Justice', writing to *The Chester-le-Street Chronicle* shortly after Sydney's case had featured in the paper, told the story of how Sydney had been 'craked' up to Bewicke Main Primitive Chapel one Sunday by some of the local ladies and youths, had then suffered the chapel being stoned and was forced to escape at the end of the service. 'Justice' argued that this was scandalous and that, though people might disagree, Sydney had the right to his opinions. It was not, perhaps, a widely held view.

In June 1916 Henry Wilson, aged 29, of Fatfield, a married builder, joiner and undertaker, appealed for exemption due to business hardship. He employed one apprentice and five bricklayers and labourers over military age. He was postponed until August. When he appeared in September he was questioned about whether he had found any 'work of National Importance', as he had apparently been instructed to do at a previous hearing. Mr Wilson stated that he had not. He was given fourteen days to find such work or he would be conscripted.

There is no H. Wilson on the St George's Roll and, presumably, that is because when the Tribunal met in October it found that it had received a certificate from Henry to the effect that he was employed as a mechanic at Harraton Colliery – work of National Importance.

In May 1916 Washington Parish Council discussed how to ensure that their clerk was totally exempted from Military Service. It seems they were successful. As the casualties continued to rise and the need for manpower grew, the council found it necessary to complain that men appearing before the tribunal in Sunderland were being asked to attend at a time prior to the arrival of the first train from Washington and, in addition, were sometimes losing a whole day's work. Why, they asked, could not Washington men be examined in Washington?

There were also those for whom an employer might appeal. **Fred Nicholson**, manager of drapery at Fatfield Co-op was exempted for six months in 1916, **Wallace Layfield**, whose appeal was made by the same Co-op, was exempted for three months and **William Taylor Dunn**, a horse-man working at Fatfield House Farm, gained an unspecified exemption. However, all three eventually served and were killed.

Fatfield Co-op.

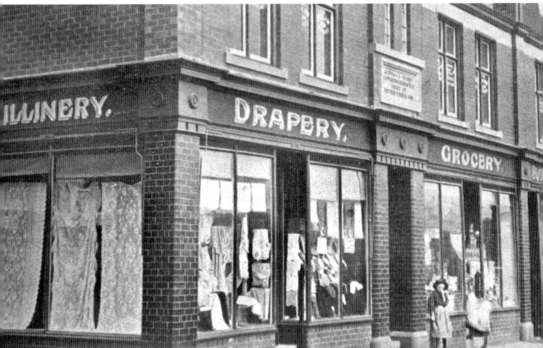

Of course the war had not been, and never was, universally popular. The class solidarity of working men, as typified by 'a bayonet is a weapon with a working man at both ends', may have been overwhelmed by the jingoism of the early days and the 'conshies' were brave to stand up, as they did, to the tide of public opinion, but they were not alone in their opposition to the war or to its effects. Thus, in August 1917, there was a meeting in Chester-le-Street, organized by the Labour Party and the National Council for Civil Liberties, at which it was asked what would be the use of England winning the war if the people who had always exploited the workers were to be allowed to do so afterwards. The only thing changed by the war, they contended, was the greater opportunity given to the profiteers to exploit the workers.

Gallipoli

Thomas Nattrass, who was killed in France in 1917, wrote a poem about the landing at Suvla Bay. It starts,

'You may talk of Balaclava
And of Trafalgar Bay
But what about the 11th Division
Who landed at Suvla Bay

And ends

And far away on the Hillside
Lying beneath the clay
Are some of the lads who died
While trying to win the day.

So remember the 11th Division
Who were all volunteers you know
And they fought and died like heroes
While going to face the foe.'

Washington lost thirteen men in the ill-favoured Gallipoli campaign – four from Harraton, five from Usworth and four from Washington Parish. Of the thirteen, only **John G Appleby** has a war grave and even then the headstone reads, 'Believed to be buried'.

JG Appleby at Lala Baba.
(Author)

Lala Baba. (Author)

Sam Holbrook was from Washington. Having enlisted on 2 November 1914, he served in the Royal Naval Volunteer Reserve as Able Seaman, Tyneside Z/878. He joined the Hawke Battalion on 10 March 1915 and was killed in action on 20 June 1915. **Sam's** name is one of those on the Helles Memorial. From his record, 'Reported by Tyneside Z/1347 AB A.Muers: "[**Sam**] Was seen on the morning of the 20th June 1915 in a Turkish Trench, lying & suffering from a severe wound in the leg." Does not think that he would have lived.' Reported by Tyneside Z/870, AB Adam Price: 'I am sorry to state he [**Sam**] got one of his legs blown off from the thigh, during the charge. He had to be left, as the order was given to retire for our lives & he would sure have bled to death.' This statement was confirmed by Tyneside Z/2732, AB John Richardson, who added, 'some men were killed trying to save **Holbrook**.' **Sam**'s death was announced on 8 July 1916, presumably because his death had now been formally accepted by the War Office.

The Royal Naval Division record states that he was living with his parents at 22 Havannah Terrace, Washington and later at Musgrave Terrace.

Hugh Murray (sometimes in documents **Hugh Morrow**) was another to die at Gallipoli, either of wounds or of dysentery. On 28 August 1916 *The Illustrated Chronicle* carried an In Memoriam: 'In loving memory of **Private Hugh Morrow**[sic], aged 20 years died 9 September 1915, dearly beloved son of John and Mary Murrow [sic],

No 1 Slate Houses, Fatfield. Had we but seen him at the last, Or watched his dying bed, Or heard the last sigh of his heart, Or held his drooping head, Our hearts, we think, would not have felt such bitterness and grief; But God has willed it otherwise and now he sleeps in peace.' **Hugh** was buried at sea on 24 September 1915, while en route to Blighty on board HMS *Valdivia*. His name appears, with those of eleven other local men, on the Helles Memorial.

Loos

In September 1915 the British attacked at Loos. Eleven Washington soldiers are named on the Loos Memorial. They are **James Leslie, John Robert Conlon, John Robert Duffy, Frank Lambert, Joseph Local, Harry Minto Nicholson, Arthur Young, Joseph Barnabas, Richard Purvis, Robert Brown** and **Harry Chilvers.** A twelfth, **George Urwin**, is buried at Dud Corner Cemetery at Loos. The battle was fought over terrain which the Washington lads, some of them having arrived in France a bare fortnight previously, would have recognized only too well – the pit heaps, colliery winding gear and rows of pit cottages in the area bear a strong resemblance to those of the North Eastern coalfield. Not only that, judging by the descriptions of life depicted in Emile Zola's, *Germinal*, the French people living in those villages could have been teleported to life in Washington and would have recognized many of its features.

In addition to those killed there were a larger number wounded. For those few in Washington whose sons had been wounded and were in hospital in France or Flanders, and were able to consider visiting them, there were regulations, simplified and re-issued in August 1915, to be followed. Only for those 'in a dangerous condition through wounds or sickness and [where] there is no military, or medical, objection to a visit being paid to him, a telegram granting permission will be sent by the War Office…' Only one relative would be allowed to visit each soldier but, should all the paperwork and hurdles have been completed and overcome, then some relatives who could not afford to pay could receive free passage. Whether anyone took up the offer…

A thirteenth local casualty at Loos was **Richard Drummond**. A corporal in 10 Battalion, Yorkshire Regiment, he died at Charing Cross Hospital in October 1922, having been wounded at Loos. On the St George's Church, Harraton, Roll of Honour he is listed as '**Drummond**

R – killed, Cooks' – a reference to Messrs Cook, Ironworks, for whom he worked. **Richard** is named on both Harraton and Washington War Memorials.

On 24 May 1916 Edith Loos Drummond was baptized at Holy Trinity Church, Usworth, her parents being **Richard** (deceased) and Mary Margaret Drummond. The Usworth Holy Trinity Church register records **Richard Drummond** (22), as marrying Mary Margaret Nagle (23), daughter of John Henry, of Coxon's Row, on 28 August 1915. A current family member states that 'Nagle' had previously been 'Schweiner' – the date of name change is unknown.

If it seems odd, macabre even, to have named 'Edith Loos' after the battle in which her father was fatally wounded, then we can note that other, similar, names relating to events of the war were given to children baptized at local churches; thus Antwerp Colpitts, Neuve Chapelle Isaac Smith, Thomas Verdun Alfred Williams and John Verdun Irwin. **George Huddart**, killed in 1917, had a daughter baptized in 1915 as Joy Aisne Smith Huddart. **Fred** and Margaret **Wilson** named a daughter Iris Alsace Lorraine. Similarly, the parents of **Robert W Taylor**, listed on the Usworth Memorial, called their house in West Hartlepool 'Zillebeke', which is where their son was killed.

In 2012 descendants of **Richard Drummond** brought into the U3A Washington War Memorials Exhibition one of the boxes from the West Indian islands of Trinidad, Grenada and St Lucia that had been used to distribute chocolates to British forces. The story they tell is that **Richard** was shot in the face at Loos and was brought to England swathed in bandages such that, when his mother went down south to visit him, she was unable to recognize him, other than by feeling his face through the bandages. When he died his body was returned by train, unloaded at Usworth Station and carried to Usworth Church on a gun carriage covered in flowers.

The box included his medals, his identity tags, a silver Usworth Parish tribute medal, the bullet which had been taken from his head, the pencil with which he used to write home, various buttons and some family photographs.

The rising death toll persuaded Harraton Parish

Richard Drummond's grave. (Family)

Drummond's chocolate box with contents. (Family)

Council to send formal letters of condolence to the parents of **Henry Wilkinson** and **Charles Todd** and, further, to agree that it would send such letters to all the families of men who were killed.

Henry Wilkinson was born in Durham, enlisted in Sunderland and was resident in Washington. He served as Lance Corporal 12414, 10 Battalion DLI and was killed on 26 June 1915, aged 20. **Henry** is commemorated on the Menin Gate at Ypres, on the St George's Roll of Honour and on both Harraton and Washington Memorials. Harraton Parish Council's letter was sent Mrs Wilkinson, of 11 Biddick Terrace, in August 1915.

Charles Todd's letter would have been delivered to the Ferryboat Inn where his father was the publican. **Charlie**, a driver in the Royal Field Artillery, was killed in August 1915 and is buried in Hop Store

Charlie Todd – seated. (Family)

Charlie Todd's plaque. (Family)

Charlie Todd's grave.
(Author)

Cemetery, close to Ypres. The plaque sent, post-war, to his parents is currently mounted on a wall in a house in Washington Village.

Of course for those soldiers overcome by fear, tension and nerves there was a remedy at hand – Dr Cassell's Tablets could make men 'Fit to Fight'; one devotee, a Gunner Jones, had taken his place in the Royal Field Artillery as a direct result of the efficacy of Dr Cassell's. At least, according to the advertisement he had.

In November 1915, in a somewhat gloomier tone, *The Durham Advertiser* carried an advertisement for Hewitt's of North Road, Durham; they were offering Ready-to-Wear Mourning. War, so it appeared, was opening up business opportunities even for those who didn't make munitions or military supplies.

The last of 1915's forty-nine war deaths [1916 would be much, much, worse] was that of **Thomas Wiseman.** The Washington and District Volunteer Record printed a list of those men who had volunteered by 8 September 1914 and one of those was **Thomas**

Wiseman, no address given. **Thomas** served as Private 14373, 10 Battalion Yorkshire Regiment. He was sent to France on 9 September 1915, survived Loos but was killed in action on 31 December 1915. He is buried in Houplines Cemetery, close to Armentières.

The War Diary of the 10th Yorkshires for 31 December 1915, reads 'Armentières: at 2.15 am an enemy patrol of three men penetrated our wire in front of listening post at House 6 and, working round the back of the post, fired on and wounded the two sentries. They escaped in the darkness.

Day quiet – weather fine but blustery. About 4 pm very heavy artillery fire and machine gun fire to which we replied.' It seems likely that **Thomas Wiseman** was one of the sentries, the only man from his battalion to die that day.

CHAPTER 6

What Did You Do in the War, Mammy?

Well, pet, pretty much what I did before the war except with less money and less food. The only thing there was more of was worrying – worrying about your Dad and your brothers and a million other things as well. Oh, and work, did I mention work? You know what they say about a woman's work? Well, in war time, it's even truer.

So what did you worry about in the war, Mammy?

What did I worry about, young lady? I worried your Dad was coming home disfigured or gassed or mad and I worried he wasn't coming home at all. I worried whether, if he got wounded, the nurses would be 'the right set of wenches to look after lads from the trenches'. I wondered if he'd be able to find a better 'ole. I worried about the war going on till Tommy and Bob were old enough to go and fight. I worried about having the money to send Daddy fags, cos Princess Mary only sent them at Christmas. And then Geordie got arrested and fined ten bob for playing cards. Ten more shillings to find. And some of his marras were only fined four bob and five bob. He must have cheeked the polis.

Was the magistrate called Dora, Mammy, or was it that Dainty Dinah?

Dainty Dinah.

Dainty Dinah footballers. (Jim Gill)

Don't be silly, pet, magistrates are always men. And Dainty Dinah, as you well know, was toffee.

Is that the toffee that's the sweetest thing on earth, Mammy? The one where they said, 'It is impossible for Tommy's girl to visit him in the trenches – but she can send Dainty Dinah as a substitute and Tommy will be glad to see her. She's the maid who couldn't make another girl jealous and she can be sent in a small tin.' That one?

That's the one, Bella. Mind you, looking at them lasses from Dainty Dinah playing football I cannit see them squeezing in a tin with their muddy boots and their pigtails, can you?

Did you have boots when you played, Mammy?

Look here, pet lamb, there might have been a war on but if you think I was going to show my legs to all those men… I mean, your Daddy had never seen my legs, never mind all them other fellas. Anyway, talking of boots – I worried about the school yard being flooded and you not having wearable boots. I also worried about being given free boots by the school or relief committee – what would people say? Then there were all those collections at school – for the Russian wounded, for soldiers' comforts, for Belgians, for the war memorials – a penny here and a penny there. Not to mention all the diseases that could carry children off. You'll remember the school was closed for measles, mumps, diphtheria and scarlet fever at various times. And then, as if we hadn't all suffered enough, the bloody Spanish sent us their influenza. You remember Thomas Huddart? Playing in the schoolyard on 4th July and died at 6 o'clock next morning. And if the diseases didn't get you, the River Wear might. Hilda Storey, remember her?

And the queues – remember when our Tommy had to stay off school because we'd heard that there were sausages at the Co-op and he turned up on a freezing cold morning to be at the front of the queue. But there were eighty-four people in front of him? And the headmaster didn't help. Weighing out the daily bread and sugar rations might have helped you understand what you were allowed but the problem was getting hold of it! And did you thank him for the recipes? He'd have been better off persuading those teachers to join up and do their bit instead of being conshies. They mightn't have thought it was right to fight the Germans, pet, but they didn't mind wreaking some violence on our Bob's hand when he was cheeky.

Worry, I'll give you worry, madam. I'll tell you what, not even Blanchard's Pills or Mother Seigel's Curative Syrup, 'unrivalled for all irregularities' could do much for my worries. Them suffragettes, they might have suffered a bit but I doubt their suffrage was like my suffrage and anyway, most of them had servants to ease their suffraging. You think Lady Lambton suffraged much in the war – I doubt it, our Bella.

I even worried about you going to see Bostock and Wombwell's menagerie. The school gave everybody the day off but, hey, those lions, they can eat children like peas off a spoon. And don't even get me started about the snakes.

And what about a woman's work, Mammy?

Just read the next few pages, pet, I've got the poss tub ready and the watter's boiled.

Worried as they undoubtedly were, the ladies of the Washington Holy Trinity Parish, according to *The Washington and District Local Advertiser*, were working fortnightly from not long after the war began. The group was directed 'energetically and ably by Mrs Lomax', [wife of the Rector of Washington Parish Church] and their minutes give a flavour of the concerns of those at home. In July 1916 the minutes included a list of the attenders – Mesdames Lomax, Humble, Vince,

Bell, Selkirk, Whiteman, Gates, Pattison and Jacques and Misses Lake, Grey, Snowdon and Potts. 'We have had a very small meeting this time, the reason being the continued pouring rain all day and many of them were waiting news of their sons from the 'Big Push' at the front as the mothers had heard they were wounded. I fear the War will cause much unsettlement to the doing of work for the Sale. It is such an anxious time.'

Some Fatfield ladies attended St John's Ambulance classes, which may have been in operation prior to the war or may have been a more recent response to the mood of everyone 'doing their bit', and then a bit more on top. In September 1916 there was a presentation evening at which a number were presented with certificates for Home Nursing and First Aid. **Dr Anderson** [died in France in 1917] gave lectures, before he went to the front, to a similar group for men.

In December 1917 the ladies of Fatfield Working Party held a successful sale of work to provide comforts for local soldiers and sailors. They were honoured by the presence of Mrs Charles Lambton.

Dr Anderson. (Permission granted from Glasgow University)

The Fatfield Sisterhood organized a concert in the Primitive Methodist Chapel on Good Friday, April 1918. Mrs Hollins presided and members and friends sang some hymns. Soloists were Mr Hall and Miss B. Cumpson, and Misses M. Scott, J. Oliver, and L. Mitford offered some recitations. Mrs D. Matthews conducted and Mrs T. Carr presided at the organ.

By June 1916 the Women's War Agricultural Committee had registered 4,893 women in County Durham. Of those women, 2,348 had experience of agricultural work and anyone wanting female labourers was invited to apply to Mrs H.M. Stobart of Harraton Hall.

As well as working on the farms, rolling bandages and looking after the ill and the maimed, some women had the chance to do work that required brains and organization. In September 1916 Mrs Walton (temporary clerk to Harraton Parish Council) stood in for her husband, Sergeant Ernest Walton, and presented lists to the local magistrates of those who were liable for jury service and those who were too poor to pay rates. [Sergeant Walton's war diary, beautifully neat and full of detail, is in Durham County Record Office.] Once he returned, however, he resumed his duties.

The need for women in the work force was highlighted in *The Chester-le-Street Chronicle* in June 1916,

'WHAT DID YOU DO?

A few weeks ago, in discussing another subject, it was pointed out in *The Chester-le-Street Chronicle* that the demand for more and more women munition workers would become much more urgent this winter. Since the article referred to was written, this fact has been very clearly pointed out in two different directions by the departments concerned.

'The Ministry of Munitions is anxious for women to enrol themselves in classes to train for munitions work at centres which it has established all over the country by arrangement with the local education authorities. The nearest one is at Rutherford Technical Institute at Newcastle and the person who should be communicated with on the subject is the Director, Mr Percival Sharp, B.Sc. The usual course extends over six weeks with four hours training each day for six days each week. The nature of the training varies according to the class of work in demand, but every effort is made to train for a special purpose. The course is divided broadly into bench work at the vice and operating machine tools, for example laths, milling machines, etc.

'Students who show marked aptitude may be selected for a further specialized course, and in such cases maintenance allowances are granted. There are excellent opportunities for such students.

'As a rule the students should be between 18 and 45 years of age, and if they are prepared to accept work in any district where there is a demand it is a decided advantage.

'Wages of not more than a sovereign to 25 shillings a week may be expected to commence with, but these increase with efficiency and hours are usually about 53 per week.

'All classes of women are invited to take advantage of this offer, but it is especially desired to train women who are not at present employed in any form of directly productive work.

'In another way a direct call is being made for women

workers who will be trained inside a certain great works, [almost certainly Armstrong-Whitworth] and who will receive wages from the very commencement.

'In this case they would have to live away from home, in buildings provided by the Government. Every arrangement is made for their food, proper meals of excellent character being provided at the appropriate hours no matter on which of the three shifts they may happen to be. Every effort is being made to care for the welfare of the workers in this new township, in the form of a great cinema, a club with reading, writing and recreation rooms, a concert hall and a dance hall. Tickets at reduced fares to any station are issued every third weekend. Particulars may be obtained by applying to the local Labour Exchange.

'It should be noted that for a woman to undertake either of these forms of work is patriotic in the highest degree, and the most urgent appeal is made to those who are not now employed in any directly productive occupation.

'Practically every man between the ages of nineteen and forty-one who is physically fit has been drafted into the army or soon will be, and when this terrible carnage is over will be able to answer with a calm face and a clear conscience, the question, "What did you do in the Great War, daddy?"

'Our women folk should take this to heart. They have been, they are, splendid, but the nation's need demands more and more from them, as it has done from the men, greater and yet greater sacrifices. Flag selling as her sole contribution to "war work" ought not to be considered sufficient for any woman who is strong enough and is not otherwise fully employed. More and more should she endeavour and more than ever before is required from her so that normal life may resume as soon as possible.'

In December 1916 the *Chronicle* carried a report about the Chester-le-Street District War Pensions Committee. 'The wife or widow or any dependant of a sailor or soldier who has served in the present war and any sailor or soldier who has so served requiring information or assistance should apply to the sub-committee; for Harraton including Fatfield its members are the Earl of Durham, Lady Anne Lambton, Mrs G. Forster and Messrs Wilson, Donkin, Tate, Sanderson, Kelly, Minto and Hall – Secretary Mr J. Donkin of Chateau, North Biddick, Washington.'

Of course it was important for those at home to try to keep spirits up in the face of the regular catastrophic news brought by telegrams, the return of wounded, disfigured or gassed soldiers and the shortage of food and other necessities. In July 1917 *The Chester-le-Street Chronicle* covered the

'LAMBTON PIC-NIC
MUNITIONETTES ENTERTAIN SOLDIERS.'

The Munitionettes may sound like a Great War rock band but their instruments were weapons of war and their tunes were the whistles of 5.9 shells; they were women employed in armaments factories and their extra contribution to the cause was, on this occasion, to give a cheerful afternoon to wounded servicemen.

'Beautiful weather, heat with a cooling breeze was vouchsaved for a most interesting picnic in Lambton Park on Saturday afternoon. One hundred and fifty munitionettes employed by Messrs Armstrong, Whitworth and Company's cartridge case shops entertained the same number of wounded soldiers from Armstrong College, Newcastle, Saltwell Towers, Gateshead and the Durham V.A.D. Hospital, together with four men from Chester-le-Street who have each lost a leg. The arrangements had been made by a committee of the workers themselves. Miss Norman, the popular Welfare Supervisor, was at the head.

'Each lady was provided with a numbered ticket and each hero was in possession of a duplicate of one of these, the idea being that the lady acted as hostess to the soldier whose ticket corresponded with her own. They had tea together and afterwards indulged in games or wandered round the park and gardens, which are at present in excellent condition, by special invitation of Lord Durham. It is worthy of remark that except in the small winter garden there are practically no flowers, all the beds being devoted to the cultivation of vegetables. During the afternoon and evening the South Pelaw Band rendered a programme of music.

'Lord Durham, who was accompanied by Lady Anne

Munitionettes. (Jim Gill)

Lambton during the afternoon, paid a visit to the field where the tea was served under the trees. The VIPs were received by Miss Norman and Mr McPherson. During tea Lord Durham, who was received with applause, said he had been approached by two young ladies who had asked him to say a few words. He had never in his life been able to resist the blandishments of young ladies and he was therefore obliged to submit to their request. It was a great pleasure to see them all there that day and to be able to express his pleasure. He was glad it was such a fine day as it was half the battle on an occasion of that kind. He would like to congratulate the ladies on the very happy thought that they should invite the wounded soldiers and heroes to come to Lambton Park. He was certain from the faces of his friends the soldiers that they quite appreciated the kindness. He hoped those that were able to go so far would avail themselves of the opportunity to go into the gardens. After nearly three years of war it was not necessary for him or any man to say what a deep debt of gratitude they all owed to the soldiers. After the war was over, and he was confident it would be successful for us, they were not going to forget the soldiers when they got out of uniform and returned to civil life. They would remember what they had done for each individual and for the country. He hoped that that day would be one of the pleasant recollections of something they had done during the war. (Applause.)'

1916 ... Summary: International Game, Sergeant Marsden Writes Home, Disabled, Discharged and Deepest Sympathy, Jutland, the Somme, Casualties,

1916 began as a year of hope. The shell shortage of 1915 had been, everyone believed, overcome; the new battalions of Kitchener's Army would go into action in the Big Push, and an Allied victory, it was hoped and assumed, was a strong possibility. The Pals' Battalions would indeed go into action on the Somme but the Big Push was to bring both casualty lists that were unimaginable and the bloodiest day in the history of the British Army. In an article printed in *The Illustrated Chronicle*, printed on 30 December 1916, General Haig offered his own, very detailed, report on the Battle of the Somme. Though aware of them, he made no comment on British casualties. By the end of the year David Lloyd George had replaced Herbert Asquith as Prime Minister.

An optimistic view of the course of the war, so far, was sent to *The Chester-le-Street Chronicle* by Mr Cooper, the words being those of his son, Private R. Cooper, then serving at the front.

'INTERNATIONAL "GAME"
FOOTBALL AND THE WAR

Great International Football Match, Britain v Germany. Teams:

Britain – Haig, Chetwood, Smith-Dorrien, McReady, Grenfell, Daniels, Prince of Wales, MacCullum, Davis, Dwyer, and O'Leary [three generals, a member of royalty, a poet, five VCs].

Germany – Kaiser, Crown Prince, Count Zeppelin, Von Hindenburg, Bernhardt, Clausewitz, Jaochin [sic], Adalbert, Von Kluck, Qomade [sic], Von Emmick.

Referee – Uncle Sam.

The match was the attraction of the century, as the two teams had not met from time immemorial. Britain brought with them to France about a million supporters of the game, and without doubt were a team to be proud of. Their second eleven were engaged in Turkey. There was a considerable delay at the outset, the Crown Prince being engaged in looting the dressing rooms. Von Kluck kicked off, and for a time Germany rather unexpectedly held their own, scoring a very doubtful goal. After great efforts to wear down the opposition (Mons), Britain rallied and some fine work by the front line brought about the equalizer (Marne). Germany blundered very badly when within shooting range (Calais) and Haig saved a very dangerous situation. After some time Britain easily obtained superiority, and Grenfell, Daniels, O'Leary, MacCullum and Davis all scored. The interval arrived with the score Britain 5 – Germany 1.

Play became very rough on the resumption, and many defenceless women and children were killed on the touchline, being crushed to death by the wild struggle of the opposition to get the ball. Zeppelin, at left back, kicked wildly, and considerable damage was done to churches and cathedrals. At length, after a desperate hand to hand struggle, Britain succeeded in capturing another goal (Neuve Chapelle). From this time onward Britain completely overwhelmed their opponents, Germany being utterly staggered. We shall lose (Loos) snivelled the Crown Prince and he was right. Goals came with astonishing number and variety, thanks to the wholehearted support of the

Allies. The whistle went with Germany thoroughly crushed and subdued. Result: Britain 12 – Germany 1 (offside). Unfortunately, the Crown Prince disappeared with the gate-money shortly before the game finished.' Britain 12 – Germany 1 – a somewhat optimistic view of the war so far.

'FATFIELD SERGEANT'S GREETINGS

Sergeant J. Marsden of Fatfield, who served in the South African War, when he was mentioned in despatches and specially promoted by Lord Kitchener for gallant services in the field, has just been invalided home from Salonika and writes from a Manchester hospital as follows: 'During my twelve months' absence in the Mediterranean, during which time I have been all round the Balkans, I have come in touch with a number of boys from my own district. They were all hale and hearty, and all looking forward for the great movement which is bound to come one of these days. I gave them a promise that I should try to let it be known that they are all gay, and wishing to be 'stuck in it' and get it over, and be nicely back to Toddy's (the Ferry Boat

The Ferry Boat Inn.

Inn) I think the Fatfield boys have played a great part right throughout the whole of the campaign. I am glad to say my trouble is only slight and my only desire is to get right and fit for France and then the finish. So far as I know I have 3 brothers in France but I have not been in touch with them. I am proud of them and hope they are quite all right.'

In fact the atmosphere at 'Toddy's' might have been somewhat subdued since the landlord's son, **Charlie Todd**, had been killed on Friday, 6 August, 1915. Another local story about 'The Ferryboat' was of the two men who, home on leave and still covered in mud, arrived at The Ferryboat Inn and paid a lad 1d to, 'pop down and tell wor lass I'll not be long'.

Disabled, discharged …. and deepest sympathy
Though losses up to this point had been unprecedented they had been light in comparison with what was to come. There was a developing recognition of the need to assist the growing number of disabled soldiers and sailors and to record local casualties. Washington Parish Council had, in November 1915, instructed the clerk to buy a suitable Roll of Honour card on which to record the names of those parishioners to fall in the war. Perhaps he purchased it from the same shop as Harraton Parish Council. Their Roll of Honour is in St George's Church and was purchased from Mawson, Swan and Morgan, Newcastle upon Tyne, though the date of purchase is not known. In February 1916 the clerk of Washington Parish Council was instructed to write to employers of different industries asking them to send representatives to a meeting to discuss ways and means of raising funds to provide Private Futers with a suitable chair and to form a suitable body to deal with similar worthy objects. *The Illustrated Chronicle* of 19 August 1915 had reported that Stephen R. Futers, 10th DLI, had been wounded. The Head Teacher's Log for Biddick Mixed School includes this entry, for 24 March 1919, 'Stephen Futers, an old boy, came into school today to ask for the loan of History books. He lost a leg in the war and is pursuing a training course at Liverpool.' [**Albert Victor Futers**, Stephen's brother, was killed in September 1916.]

Barmston and Usworth Parish Councils were invited, in March 1916, to join Washington Parish in schemes for assisting the disabled and the honouring of 'Distinguished Heroism'. A meeting took place in April but no details were offered in any council minutes.

Correspondence collected by Chester-le-Street Poor Law Union about 'Discharged soldiers applying for outdoor relief', made reference to 'Martin Guy, 7th Yorks. Enlisted November 1914 and was wounded in France in October 1915. He was shot in the stomach and the bullet passed out below his heart. Discharged 8/7/16 as medically unfit and has received no pay since then. Has tried to work but finds he is unable to do so. He has been relieved in kind and the case is being brought before the Military Authorities.' Martin's diary notes laconically for 25th October, 'Listening post, Hooge trenches, wet. Shot. Popperinge (sic) hospital.' [After the war Martin became Chairman of the Usworth and New Washington Social Centre, an organization set up to help the unemployed; he also became involved in spiritualism after, the story goes, his wife showed him she was able to move plates on the wall.]

Martin Guy. (Family)

Another case was that of, '**John Thomas Douglas**, a miner, attested, aged forty-two and died in Newcastle Infirmary on 30th April 1916. Was sent home sick and received army pay up to the time of his death. Pay and allotment of pay ceased for his wife and four children from that date and nothing has been received since. Relieved in kind. This woman has a son in the army aged 19 from whom she receives 3/6d per week.' **John T Douglas**, of 16 Glen Terrace had attested on 9 September 1915 and became a private in the Army Service Corps. His Pension Record notes that he was suffering from 'aortic stenosis and aneurism of arch' and that his condition had been pre-existing but aggravated by army service. It was not noted how, or if, he had been helped but at least there was some recognition that something needed to be done for these men and their families.

Washington Parish Council had time to ask the clerk to convey their deepest sympathy to Mr and Mrs Robert Varley, the cemetery superintendent, 'on the loss of their son in France'. Originally, **Benjamin Redhead Varley** had enlisted in the Tyneside Irish. On 23 March 1916 **Bartholomew**'s father wrote to the War Office, 'Dear Sir, My son **B.R. Varley** 9528 34th Division Army Cyclist Corps was killed on 16th March 1916 and up until the present time I have received nothing in the way of personal belongings and he had quite a number in his pockets and on his person. I will be extremely obliged if you will forward everything or anything which he had on his person at the time, Yours faithfully, R.J. Varley.'

On 10 July Mr Varley wrote again, 'Colonel Cycling Records, Hounslow. Dear Sir, I beg to acknowledge the receipt of spectacles in case, identity disc, soldiers' small book and prayer book, being the personal belongings of my dear son.'

Bartholomew's family received the plaque and scroll in March 1919 and his War and Victory medals in July 1921. The Roll of Honour drawn up for Washington and Barmston Parishes included **Bartholomew Redhead Varley** and gave his address as 10, Musgrave Terrace.

The Holy Trinity Parish magazine for April 1916 included the following, 'The war has again levied its cruel toll upon some of the homes in the parish. **Alfred James Robson, John Wake, Bartholomew Redhead Varley** and **John George Todd** have laid down their lives for their country. Two of them were married and two single. Each of them has left behind those who deeply mourn their loss. I remember most vividly seeing one of them go down to the station after his last furlough full of the hope and promise of life, and now he has passed with his comrades into another life and world. "Toll for the brave, the brave that are no more." I think it right and fitting that the Church that prayed for them in life should remember them in death, therefore I propose to honour their memory and sacrifice at the Evening service on the 4th Sunday in Lent, that is, April 2nd. To those whom they have left bereaved we tender our sympathy, our most heartfelt sympathy. It is not easy to say what we feel on these occasions but I know that I can assure them of our desire that God our Father be with them in all love and presence and power to help them in large measure in this their great sorrow.'

Jutland

Of the 400 Washington men killed in the Great War only five were in the Navy. They were **Thomas Scorer, Ernest W Coxon, Frank Embleton, William J Ball** and **William Carl Routledge.** The latter was born on 17 March 1897 in Newcastle but was living in South Shields at the time of the 1901 Census. By 1911 the family had moved to Washington. **William C** joined the Navy in January 1916, for the length of hostilities [the army called it 'for the duration']. He was a fitter and underwent training on HMS *Victory II* before taking up his role as M/18678, Wireman Second Class, on HMS *Defence*, a cruiser, sunk with all hands [903 men] during the Battle of Jutland, 31 May 1916. **Wireman Routledge** is commemorated on the Portsmouth Naval Memorial. His naval record indicates that his parents were paid a war gratuity but the amount is not stated.

Electrician **C Routledge**, Royal Navy, is commemorated on the plaque to those members of the Westwood Social Club who either served or served and died in the Great War.

In the Holy Trinity Church Parish magazine for July 1916 we find this, 'The Naval battle off the coast of Jutland has thrilled and stirred the nation. At first a feeling of dismay seized the hearts of the people owing to the first official statement issued by the Admiralty. Those in authority have been blamed for mishandling the situation. Well, at any rate there was no need to retract from their first statement. They were straight about our own losses, and they were careful not to say more than they were at first sure of about the losses of the foe. Compare this with the untruthful methods of our opponents. The ships that have been lost can be replaced, but the lives of the great and glorious dead, never again in this world. Washington contributed at least one who died in the engagement – **William Carl Routledge** went down with the *Defence*, Admiral Arbuthnot's flagship. **Routledge** had only just been transferred from another boat to the *Defence*. He was only five months in the Navy but during that time had made headway and because of his work and ability was sent to the *Defence*. We think of him with pride and gratitude, and we pray that he may rest in peace until the day when there shall be no more sea. To his parents we desire to extend our heartfelt sympathy. They have another son serving in the Navy.'

The Somme

A headline in *The Illustrated Chronicle* of 4 July 1916 was '**LOSSES LIGHT**'. The article had this to say about the Battle of the Somme that had started three days previously with the loss of 60,000 British casualties, about 20,000 of them killed, 'The losses of the British and French troops in the great battle of the Somme have been extraordinarily light. I am able to make this statement on the authority of a high military personage and have supplemented the information by the evidence of my own eyes.' The writer was H.J. Greenwall of the *Daily Express*. He went on to describe the scene,

'The barrage was as if all the demons of the nether regions had escaped and were filling the air with their lamentations.

'Amid the terrible din the men lay down, with their knapsacks on, and had a meal of bread, cheese and sardines. Afterwards came the order to stand to arms and they began filing into the trenches. Suddenly a whistle was blown and a whispered command was passed along the ranks to fix bayonets…'

Perhaps Mr Greenwall had been further away from the German machine guns than the soldiers of whom he wrote. A German view of events at Beaumont Hamel on 1 July was, 'We dusted them off good'. Sadly, that was more accurate than Mr Greenwall's view.

On 1 July 1916 fourteen men from Usworth, sixteen from Washington and ten from Harraton were killed as the battle opened. Before the end of the week another seven had suffered the same fate and by the end of July another seventeen had perished. At least sixty-four local men died in July 1916.

Those killed on 1 July were, according to the *Commonwealth War Graves Commission*: **Joseph Affleck, James Drummond, Thomas Hall, Thomas Hayton, John M Hunter, Thomas Jeffrey, Henry Lewins, Henry Marriner, John G Pepper, Henry Shields, Thomas Todd, David Trotter, William Troupe, Thomas Mallaburn, James Armstrong, John H McLahaney, Thomas McCrerey, John G Pearson, Thomas Penaluna, Thomas Pluse, Henry Simpson, George B Smith, Alfred Wilkinson, Ralph Atkinson, John W Cook, John Gilmaney, Edgar Helm, Ralph J Hopson, Richard O Laws, Thomas Donaldson, Robert Boyle, James Nicholson, James G**

Oliver, Thomas Walker, Henry Wells, Robert Willis, Charles Jeffrey, Thomas Foster, Henry Fletcher and **Benjamin Doyle.** Twenty-two of the forty killed on 1 July are among the 72,000 men listed on the Thiepval Memorial to the Missing of the Somme.

Casualties

Thomas Cowell was the first Washington man to die in 1916. He had been a miner at F Pit before enlisting on 5 September 1914 and serving in 2 DLI. His battalion was in reserve at Poperinghe for the first four days of January 1916 but moved up to the line to relieve the West Yorkshires on 5 January, the Battalion War Diary recording very heavy shelling, which may account for **Tommy**'s death. By the time Mrs Cowell received **Tommy**'s effects [not listed in his record] she was living at Wallsend-on-Tyne and, when asked to complete a list of his relatives after the war, she wrote on the form, 'Don't know nothing about relatives'. She received a pension of 10s per week.

From *The Illustrated Chronicle*, '**Scott**, died in France, through gas poisoning, 4 July 1916, aged twenty-seven. **Private Herbert Scott**, Northumberland Fusiliers, beloved husband of E.A. Scott, Waggonway Terrace, Fatfield. His pleasant face and kindly ways are pleasant to recall. He had a loving word for each and died beloved by all. Though buried in a distant grave amidst the shot and shell, For his country he gave his life, he stood his trials well. No matter how I think of him, no matter how I call, There's nothing left to answer but his photo on the wall. Forget the hours reminders bring, The songs he loved, the books he read, Forget my hand now bears his ring, Which binds me loving to him dead. Sadly missed and deeply mourned by his sorrowing wife and children and friends. Service in St George's Church, Fatfield, August 6th at 6 pm. All friends kindly invited.'

Herbert's first enlistment took place at Shiney Row in August 1914 when he became 33746, Royal Regiment of Artillery. He was twenty-six, and a miner, born in Felling. However, he was only in the army for twenty-four days, being discharged as not likely to become an efficient soldier, though no reason was given. *The Chester-le-Street Chronicle* of 5 February 1915 reported that **H Scott,** of 2 Waggonway Terrace, had joined the Tyneside Scottish. **Herbert** was not alone in joining, being discharged and then re-joining, usually with a different regiment.

Herbert Scott. (Family)

William Jonas – football medals. (Family)

William Jonas. (Steve Jenkins,
Leyton Orient Supporters' Club)

William Jonas was born in Cambois, Northumberland, in 1891, one of ten children of William and Elizabeth. By 1911 the family was living in Usworth and **William**, a good footballer, was playing, and scoring lots of goals for, Havannah Rovers. He was transferred to Clapton Orient and became one of the forty-one players and staff to enlist, joining the BEF in France on 17 November 1915. He was killed in action on 27 July 1916 and is commemorated on the Thiepval Memorial.

From the book, *'The Greater Game; Sporting Icons Who Fell in the Great War',* by Clive Harris and Julian Whippy: 'On the Somme just weeks later, 17 Middlesex took part in costly actions in Delville Wood in late July. **F/32 Private William Jonas** was killed on 27 July along

Havannah Rovers. (Holbrook/Grainger family)

Memorial to William Jonas at Flers. (Author)

with nine colleagues. **Jonas**, a Northumberland lad, had made his debut for (Clapton) Orient in 1912 after an impressive goal tally for Havannah Rovers. A skilful player known for the quality of his passing, he had a turn of speed that frequently frustrated opposing defenders who were happy to chop him down in full flight. Adaptable and fully committed to his team, he once played in goal at Nottingham Forest after regular goalkeeper Jimmy Hugall – a comrade in 17 Middlesex who would survive the war to play again – was injured. **Jonas** was a pin-up of Orient's female support, it has been suggested he received up to fifty letters a week from admirers which led him to announce his happy marriage [to Mary Jane] in the club programme.'

He was once sent off for fighting with the Millwall goalkeeper in an FA Cup tie at The Den. Incensed, the home crowd took to the field and only mounted police and an escort back to East London saved the Orient players and supporters.

In 2008 Leyton Orient Supporters' Club made a visit to the Somme and have subsequently raised money, including by the sale of lapel badges, to have a memorial built to Richard McFadden, **William Jonas** and George Scott, the three Orient players killed in the Great War. A descendant of **William Jonas** has a locket with photographs of **William** and Mary Ann and also a football medal for winning the BEF 2nd Division Cup, 1915–16 season. Two of **William's** descendants were invited to lay a wreath on the pitch at Loftus Road for the Leyton Orient Remembrance Service in 2012.

Forty-one Washington men died on 1 July and we can assume that many more were wounded. One such was Thomas 'Tipper' Willcocks, who lost an eye at the Somme and had it replaced with a bakelite blue eye. His daughter recalls being taken to the Ferryboat Inn (Toddy's) when aged about nine and her Dad telling her to sit quietly while he went to talk to someone at the bar. He took his eye out, put it on the table and said to it, 'Keep an eye on me pint'. Tipper died in the 1950s but his eye was not buried with him. His daughter took it from the pillow as he was laid out and kept it in a small box filled with cotton wool and with fake pearls stuck on the top. As she tells the story, no one knew what she'd done until she fell over in the back yard, lost the box from her pinny pocket and, crying with scraped knees and the panic of loss, was found by her mother, crawling about in the snow, searching. 'What on earth are you doing, our Brenda?'

Tipper Willcocks.
(Brenda Burns)

Tipper's medal and eye. (Brenda Burns)

'Looking for my Dad's eye.' 'You what?'

When the eye was found her mother said, 'Lawks-a-daisy, our Brenda, where did you get that?' Brenda still has her Dad's eye and his Silver War Badge and holds them, one in each hand, at 11.00 am each Remembrance Day.

The last of the, approximately, 135 Washington soldiers and sailors to be killed in 1916 was **William Robinson** of Orchard House, who, when he enlisted in December 1915, was twenty-nine years old, a single cartman. He was mobilized in February 1916, becoming Private 30857, 3 DLI. At the time of his death, 4 December 1916, he was Private 20926, 12 Duke of Wellington's (West Riding Regiment).

Private Robinson joined the BEF in France on 1 April 1916 and was killed by the explosion of a grenade while digging in a trench. A Court of Inquiry was held into his death and the wounding, in the same incident, of Privates Wilkinson, 12/21737, and Harney, 12/20332. Private Wilkinson told the inquiry, 'In a working party all three men were of the West Riding Regiment. About 10 am I heard a loud explosion about fifty yards away. I found **Private Robinson** lying on his back. There was a hole in his forehead. His heart stopped beating about three minutes after the explosion and in my opinion he was then dead. He was not conscious after the explosion.' He went on, 'I saw immediately after the explosion **Private Robinson**. He was hit in or near the eyes by some substance from the explosion. I did not know that Private Harney had also been hit until about 2 pm.'

The author of the report continued, 'Some pieces of newly burst Mills grenade were found about on the ground after the explosion. The deceased and the two injured men were working with spades at the time of the explosion. In my opinion the accidental hitting of a Mills grenade by a spade caused the explosion. The work was in the bottom of an old trench.'

At the time he enlisted, **William**'s next of kin was his mother, Jane, but, by the time of his death, the list of relatives stated that he had no living mother or father and that his siblings were Joseph, at Orchard House, Thomas Harold, serving in the MTC [perhaps the Motor Transport Corps] in London, and Jane Mary, at Orchard House.

Private Robinson's effects were sent home in June 1916 and his family received his plaque and scroll in May 1919 and his War and Victory medals in May 1921.

CHAPTER 8

1917 ... Summary: USA Joins In, Belgian Morality and Rations, Recipes and Food Orders, Allotments, School Strike, J.W. Cook's, Casualties

1917 saw the slog continue on the Western Front; Arras, Passchendaele, Messines Ridge and Cambrai were added to the list of battles; the Germans began unrestricted submarine warfare; there were two revolutions in Russia and mutinies in the French Army. If there was a ray of hope, it came in April when, among others, *The Chester-le-Street Chronicle* reported,

'AMERICA JOINS IN NEW PAGE OF HISTORY

A new page in the world's war has been opened. President Wilson has placed the unsheathed sword of freedom into the hands of the people of the United States of America.

He has told them it is their duty to take it up and fight for the cause of liberty and Democracy, the unfettered popular government of the peoples of the world and the permanent overthrow of despotism, autocracy, militarism and Prussianism – in all its forms of cunning, greed, secret espionage and plotting – which have caused the war.

It is not the German people that decided for war, he said, but the autocratic and military caste under which they are yoked and shackled.

He outlined the violation of Belgium, the U-boat piracy and murders, denouncing them in scathing terms, and the defiance of international law and usage, and said U-boats, if dealt with at all, must be dealt with on sight.

The entry of the United States no doubt gave morale a boost but it would not be until the summer of 1918 that the doughboys began to play any significant part on the Western Front. Indeed, with Russia descending into revolution, the spring of 1918 would see the Allies retreating, again, as the Germans launched their last attempts at a military victory.

In July 1918 Chester-le-Street Rural District Council received a letter from the British-American fellowship on the subject of forming an organization to extend hospitality to American soldiers. It was agreed to issue posters asking for accommodation for American soldiers who wished to visit the district. Whether any ever did...

So, the Americans were coming...but the Belgians were already here and their presence raised some issues.

The Belgians in Birtley

At the outbreak of the Great War, Britain was faced with a munitions shortfall. More factories were needed to provide armaments and in July 1915 an agreement was made between the government and the Armstrong-Whitworth Company to build two factories at Birtley, one to produce shells, the other cartridge cases. As nearly all able-bodied men were otherwise engaged, the Belgian government in exile was contacted. This resulted in an agreement between the British and Belgians in February 1916, whereby the Belgian administration agreed to manage the factories and provide all of the necessary labour while the British paid all expenses and materials. The workforce for these factories was to be made up solely of Belgian refugees and wounded Belgian servicemen and so Elisabethville, named after the Queen of Belgium, was born, a complete, self-contained, small town to house these Belgian workers. It was built to house a total of 3,000 men. Once the war ended, the Belgian refugees returned to their home country and Elisabethville was then used for Birtley families.

In August 1917 *The Chester-le-Street Chronicle* carried a story about the Belgians, headed '**LOCAL MORALITY**'. A letter was read to the Rural District Council meeting from the Chief Constable of Durham who was asking that a certain section of the Town Police Clauses Act should be adopted in the parishes of Lamesley, Birtley, Harraton, Ouston and Pelton. Under the subheading, **'MAGISTRATE'S OPINION OF BELGIANS',** the article continued, 'Mr Mole said as a magistrate he could see, and many of those present could see, that something would have to be done. The Belgians at Birtley were becoming an absolute nuisance to the whole of the community of the district. At every sitting of the Police Court three quarters of the time was taken up in considering the immoral offences of the Belgians. They must do something to prevent this for the sake of their children.'

[*The Chester-le-Street Chronicle* carried regular stories of Belgians breaking curfews, Belgians being involved in paternity suits, Belgians living out of their enclave without reporting to the police etc. For example, in October 1917 Edith McLean, 20, and Elizabeth Wilson, 25, both from Newcastle were charged with having been in the Belgian Colony during prohibited hours and fined 20s. Two Belgian men were charged with aiding and abetting, found guilty and sentenced to a month's hard labour, a fine of £5 each and the cost of an interpreter's fees.]

'The Chairman said he did not want to blame all Belgians. There were Belgians and Belgians. The same would probably take place if we, as Britishers, were driven from our own homes into a foreign land. There would be some of us, and there would be others. [Presumably he said this with a particular look on his face, perhaps a nod and wink as well.]

'Mr Wilson, Edmondsley, said it was the women who came from Newcastle, Durham, Gateshead and other places who caused the trouble mostly. It was not so much the Belgians.

'Mr Cullen said they ought to consider closely whether they should give away their liberty so easily. If certain sections [of the Police Act] were put into operation it would be impossible for 2 men to meet and discuss their work. They should not come to rash conclusions because they had discovered for the first time that there were prostitutes in England.

'Mr Mole said he questioned that. The trouble was that a great number of women who had hitherto been decent were being prostituted by these chaps because the men have a lot of money.

'The Chairman said he wanted to prevent some of our most decent women being tempted off the straight path by the lure of gold while their husbands were away fighting. A small committee was appointed to meet the Chief Constable and Inspector Gargate.'

Well, morality was one concern – the issue of food supplies affected everyone and the quality and extent of Belgian rations was a topic that caused doubt, suspicion and anger.

'SUGAR SMUGGLING
Food committee's strong statements
'DOWN TOOLS' POLICY THREATENED
Co-operative Store Warned

'A meeting of the Chester-le-Street Rural Food Control Committee was held on Thursday [1 March 1918], over which Mr E. Cook presided. Mr T. Hitch and Mr R.E. Hale, representing the Food Commissioner, waited on the committee in respect to the Belgian Colony.

'The Chairman began by stating that the Committee had come to the conclusion that there must be food control for Belgian and Briton alike. He proposed to make a few statements as to what was going into the canteens at the Belgian Colony in Birtley. This was quite apart from any other works whatever and from the Belgian Colony itself. On a certain recent date truckloads of sugar were absolutely smuggled into the Colony by the railway siding instead of being brought through the streets and it was emptied by the Belgians themselves. This could be proved by the vouchers of the North East Railway Company. With regard to the canteens alone he had a statement extending over four months as to certain foodstuffs which had been received. They knew that men who were rationed at Newcastle, Gateshead and elsewhere could go into the canteens and have ham or bacon and eggs for breakfast and a cut of the sirloin for dinner and that they were prepared to pay whatever was asked.

They could then go to Newcastle where they were rationed and get another dinner there.

'Mr Hitch said the Belgians were rationed.

'Mr Cook said they had all heard that statement until it was absolutely threadbare. They found there was no truth in it. If they were rationed inside the Colony the committee wanted to know how it was they could get two substantial meals in the canteens.

CANTEEN SUPPLIES

'Mr Cook then proceeded to give figures for certain dates in November. The figures referred to comprised large quantities of beef and mutton from various sources, bags of hams, bread from Alnwick, tins of biscuits and other things.'

'The Chairman then produced a long list of foodstuffs sent in to the colony, making it clear that the amounts seemed very generous. Mr Hitch, defensively, stated that there were 6,000 Belgians.

'Mr Mole said, 'These Belgians were making from £12 to £19 per fortnight, while miners in the same district were making from £2.10s.0d to £3 per fortnight. With all this money to spend it was no wonder that they were forcing up the cost of living in the district.

'Mr Craggs said the previous Thursday he went home from the pit to a kipper.

'The Chairman said the Belgian ordered ham and eggs or bacon and eggs at breakfast and got them.

'Mr Craggs said it had come to the position that if this sort of thing continued something would happen amongst the workmen at Washington.

'The Chairman said he had not had a piece of bacon in his house for eight weeks and not a living soul had heard him grumble. He was prepared to stand everything if everyone else stood the same thing. But he was not going to stand the Belgian having ham and eggs for his breakfast and having ham and eggs at home.

'Mr Handy said in the Usworth district there was a coal hewer named _____ who worked five days without meat and when Sunday came he had corned beef for dinner... If the authorities were not prepared to consider what impression was being created with regard to the Colony in the districts immediately adjoining it, they would soon find if something was not done that a much larger number of policemen would be required. Because if they, as miners, were going to be without meat, and these people for whom they were having to provide a shelter were to have meat, there would be force used, and that would be the worst thing that could happen. The people who were being sheltered must be amenable to the same shortage as the people of the country.

'Mr Wilson (Harraton) said that day he had gone home to half a pound of black pudding to be divided between four persons. They were not getting anything like what they should have.

'The Chairman said the existing condition of things made a man's blood boil. He knew a young woman who worked in a munitions factory from patriotic motives who had gone to work that day with dry bread. The groceries for his own household of three persons for a fortnight had come to 4/9d. He could not get anything else.

'Mr Handy said their attitude to the Belgians should be one of sympathy but under the circumstances that was impossible. They were getting big wages, getting well fed and were corrupting as many women as they could. The whole Colony was becoming a stinking den of iniquity.'

A fortnight after this lively discussion, Mr Gibb, representing the Ministry of Munitions, refuted allegations about Belgian rations. He said that people ought to check facts before making such allegations.

Recipes
In order to help those who needed ideas for menus and diets *The Chester-le-Street Chronicle* consulted E.I. Spriggs, M.D., F.R.C.P., acting on behalf of the Food Controller, and he offered the following advice to those struggling to feed their families. 'The ingredients would produce for the Plain Diet about 2,500 calories per day and a protein intake of about 3½ ounces at a cost of 8/8d per person per week – 15 lbs of bread, 7 lbs of flour, 10 lbs of meat, 2 lbs of sugar, 2½ lbs of

fish, and then oatmeal, dripping, lentils, barley, rice, beans, potatoes, vegetables, tea, syrup, cocoa, stock, eggs, milk, margarine.' The selection of suggested dishes included boiled eggs, boiled mutton with white sauce, treacle pudding, mutton pie, tapioca pudding, hot-pot, broth, potted meat, curried mince, beefsteak pie, stewed mutton, lentil soup, kedgeree, curried fish, stewed liver and onions and cold mutton. As the writer pointed out there was no meat on Fridays and the amounts of rationed food per head were 3 lbs of flour, 2½ lbs of meat and ½ lb of sugar.

The medium diet would cost about 1s/9d per week more and included, in addition to the items listed above, kippers, cheese, butter, fruit, jam, jelly and marmalade. The medium dishes that were suggested were oatcake and barley scones, stuffed mutton, macaroni cheese, fish soup, boiled sausages, milk puddings, cold tongue, lentil soup, ginger pudding, custard and dates, fish cakes, curried mutton, jellied beef and beetroot, mutton cutlets, Irish stew, apple dumpling, and beef mould.

The third diet contained more expensive foods, with the object of leaving the cheaper foods for the more needy, and the amounts were for a household of eight, including children and servants. Ingredients not mentioned in the other diets included sausage, bacon, salmon, stilton cheese, flaked maize, parsnips, greens, carrots, honey, coffee, biscuits, tinned and dried fruits and oranges. The servants could be knocking up fish soup, boiled beef, pancakes with oranges and sugar, rice mould, peaches, sirloin, beans, Brussels sprouts and Yorkshire pudding, fish pie, fig pudding, blanc-mange, stewed apples and spice pudding.

Food orders

If the government could insist that men went to fight then it could also regulate many other aspects of people's lives and behaviour. In August of 1917 Chester-le-Street Rural District Council, under the heading of the DORA Act, made some announcements in which the assistance of the public was requested. The list of Food Orders was long: Brewers Sugar Order, Price of Milk Order, Feeding of Game Order, Sugar (Confectionery) Order, Bread Order, Swedes (Prices) Order, Food (Conditions of Sale) Order, Tea (Nett Weight) Order, Manufacture of Flour and Bread Order, Public Meals Orders (three in number), Cake and Pastry Order, Wheat, Rye and Rice (Restriction) Order, Maize, Barley and Oats (Restriction) Order, Horse (Rationing) Order, Beans, Peas and Pulses (Retail Process) Order, Meat (Sales) Order and Sugar (Domestic Preserving) Order. Anyone wanting details of the above orders was asked to send 1s/5d to H.M. Stationery Office. Mr T.S. Wadge, Sanitary Inspector, of Station Rd, Washington, was the man to whom breaches of the Orders should be notified, if such breaches occurred in Barmston, South Biddick, Bournmoor, Harraton, Little Lumley, Lambton, Usworth or Washington. What the RDC was seeking was information about anyone breaching the above Orders in the following ways: 'the waste of wheat, rye, rice and the flour made therefrom; the feeding of game birds with grain or other foodstuffs, the sale of bread baked for less than twelve hours; the sale of any currant, sultana or milk bread; the use of sugar in bread-making; the sale of bread other than by weight; the sale of bread except it be of one pound or an even number of pounds in weight; the sale of any bread roll except it weigh not less than 1 ounce; the trading of any tapioca, sago, manioc or arrowroot except for human consumption; the sale of any type or derivative of maize for more than 3½d per pound, the sale of any derivative of oats at more than 5d per pound, the use of any oats, maize, beans, cereals for feeding horses over and above what was allowed; the sale of beans, pulses and lentils at above their specified prices [between 6d and 9d per pound]; the sale or offer for sale or the possession of for the purposes of sale crumpet, muffin, teacake or fancy bread or light and fancy pastries or any cake bun scone or biscuit which had anything added to the dough after mixing or during or after baking; the sale of, or offer to sell, chocolate at more than 3d per ounce; the use of any sugar or chocolate for covering cakes, pastries, or other like articles and the sale, or offer of sale, of any such article; the sale of sugar issued by the Sugar Commission for domestic fruit preserving for any other purpose; the attempt to impose in connection with the sale of any article of food any condition relating to the purchase of any other article; the sale or offer for sale of milk at more than 2d per imperial quart; the sale of Swedes, or Swedish turnips, at a price (including the cost of packaging) exceeding 1½d per pound; the sale by retail of any tea in quantities of 2 oz or over except by nett weight in ounces or pounds or in multiples of ounces or pounds; the sale of dead meat at more than 3d per stone (of 8 lbs) above the cost to the vendor of the meat sold.'

As the RDC pointed out, 'Any infringement of any order is a summary offence under the Defence of the Realm Regulations and renders the offenders on conviction liable to imprisonment for 6 months with or without hard labour or a fine of £100 or both.' The Allies were fighting for Freedom, Democracy, Justice and the Right to Regulate Civilians to Within an Inch of their Lives.

Allotments

Back in September 1914 Barmston Parish Council received a letter from the Board of Agriculture with leaflets suggesting that gardens and allotments ought to be cultivated. In February 1918 Barmston Council agreed to put up notices at Washington Chemicals informing workmen that allotments were available. There is no evidence of anything happening between those dates but, in May 1916, Harraton Parish Council discussed requests it had received for allotments. They agreed to approach the Earl of Durham, through his agent, Mr Gray, to see if land could be made available and under what conditions. By March 1917, after some tetchiness about the location and quality of the land offered and the prices demanded, the first allotments were pegged out beside Wormhill Terrace, The Parade and Biddick Terrace. Durham County Council's Land Agent had been involved as had Mr Kirkup of Lambton and Hetton Collieries. Decisions then had to be made about rules for allotment holders, the rents to be charged and the length of leases. It is just possible that before the war ended food was grown on these plots but, as can be seen, the situation had dragged on for a long time. By June 1917 Harraton's Allotment Committee consisted of Messrs Wilson, Kay, Oliver, McArtin and Baker and they had all kinds of problems to deal with. One man who had taken an allotment decided that it was not in a good enough condition to work and the council had to decide whether he had to be held to his tenancy and charged the rent. Another built a stable on his land and it took the council some months of persuasion to get it removed.

Concurrent with these negotiations, other events were in motion. In May 1917 Messrs Ayton and Houston attended the HPC meeting and said the 'food question' was becoming serious and asked the council to form a sub-committee to encourage people to use substitutes instead of flour. In July 1917 the council moved that Durham County Council be asked to put the 'Feeding of School Children Act' into force in Fatfield schools as the pits were working so badly. In August 1917 DCC replied that Harraton Council had to forward their recommendations to the County Education Committee and so, in September, they wrote to Mr Dickinson at the DCC Education Committee asking that this should happen.

As early as September 1914 Usworth Council Mixed School's headmaster had noted in his Log Books that 'feeding of necessitous children' had taken place. Breakfasts and dinners had been served at the Miners' Hall 'to the children of workers at Washington Colliery, which has worked very little since the commencement of the war and the call-up of reservists'. This continued until November 1914.

On 19 November 1917 the headmaster of Usworth Council Mixed School wrote in his log, 'A school strike has commenced and very few children attended school. Yesterday morning a mass meeting of miners of the district was held in the Alexandra Theatre, New Washington, to consider how to get more work or more relief. As a protest against the alleged delay or inaction of the Education Committee in not yet providing meals for the children it was agreed that all schoolchildren should be kept from school pending further developments.' On 21 November he wrote, 'The strike is over. The maximum relief obtainable per family was yesterday raised and school feeding is for the present considered unnecessary. Accordingly, after a meeting held last night, the local "crakeman" went round parts of the district declaring the strike ended. The Head teachers of the district have sent in their resignations from the Washington and Usworth Relief Committee.'

The story, as reported in *The Sunderland Echo*, noted the meeting at the Alexandra and added, 'The children of nine schools are affected. They are to be kept from school until the Act is put into operation.

'It was announced that Sir Richard Redmayne, Chief Inspector of Mines, is to visit the North to inquire into the distribution of the coal trade in in Durham County and to try to secure a better allocation of orders.' Three days later –

'SCHOOL STRIKE ENDED IN WASHINGTON DISTRICT

The school strike in the Washington and Usworth district, which was declared on Monday, has been settled, and today the juvenile strikers returned to their studies. In two days these youngsters, by making their fathers' cause their own, have achieved a decisive victory and secured concessions for which their elders have been clamouring for some time.

'The terms of the settlement were arranged in Durham yesterday. A deputation from the Chester-le-Street Board of Guardians, consisting of Mr Eli Cook (chairman), Mr T. Craggs (Washington), Mr Miles Handy (Usworth), and Mr R.V. Dickinson (clerk) waited upon a specially convened meeting of the Durham County Prince of Wales Fund Committee in the Shire Hall, and put the miners' case. They were accorded a sympathetic hearing, and finally the committee agreed that the maximum income of families eligible for relief from the Fund should be raised from 24s to 27s per week. This maximum of 27s will not include the Coal Controller's award of 9s weekly, nor the money received by the men from the Durham Miners' Association, nor the earnings of boys. This means that no family, however slack work may be at the pits, will have less than £2.1s.0d per week coming into the house. Hence, it will not now be necessary to put into operation the Feeding of the School Children Act, which was the object of the school strike.

REAL SUFFERING

'The concessions granted by the Durham County Prince of Wales' Fund Committee will have the effect of banishing the spectre of want from the Washington district. That want was being experienced by many families in the district is incontrovertible. Our representative made careful and thorough inquiries in Washington and its environs, and the facts brought to light lead him to the conclusion that, unfortunately the miners' statement that many families are practically starving is not exaggerated. As is generally known, for some little time past – from four to six months – there has been very little work at the collieries in and around Usworth and Washington. In fact, whereas an ordinary week's work should consist of five shifts, the men latterly have been working only two and a half shifts per week – sometimes less, and, as a consequence, the miners' weekly wages have averaged not more than about 26s – in some cases much lower. The result has been that, food prices being so high, many of the men have been unable to buy sufficient of the necessaries of life to feed themselves, their wives and their families. Of course the suffering is not universal to the district, but it is undoubtedly considerable, particularly where there are large families, and the miner's family is usually a large one. Some of the children really do look pinched and underfed, and large numbers are either without boots or possessed of very bad ones.

'Our representative's enquiries were not confined to the miners. Schoolmasters and teachers, whose position enables them to judge impartially, stated that there was undoubtedly much suffering in the district. Some of the children bore undoubted signs of mal-nutrition, and nearly all the teachers had personal knowledge of one or two families which were subject to great privation. Two significant signs were that the pawnshops are, and have been for some time past, very busy and grocers and other traders have stopped credit.'

A Salvation Army officer with knowledge of the area was then quoted about the lack of boots and food in the area before the report continued, 'The strike began on Monday, and at least a thousand youngsters were affected. It was most general in Usworth, where the size of various classes was reduced to what an educational reformer would call ideal proportions, one teacher having under his or her charge between two and half a dozen children. In New Washington about 75 per cent of the children were absent from school, but in Old Washington the average attendance was between 50 and 60 per cent, since many of the workers there are not dependent on the collieries.'

The Echo then told the story of a non-striker who'd been verbally abused by striking children shouting, 'Blackleg! Blackleg!! Scallywag!!!', and ending with the dreaded 'Cowardy-cowardy-custard!'

The report ended with comments by 'Coun. Timothy McQuire, of the Usworth Lodge, who was the mover of the resolution to initiate a school strike. "It isn't that we won't work," he said. "Whenever the manager has wanted us we went gladly. We can't get the work, and things came to such a pass that we simply had to call a school strike to get the Government to feed our children. Either the Government must distribute the coal orders fairly, so that we can earn enough to keep body and soul together, or they must feed our children now that the poverty they have forced upon us has come. We would prefer to work, we don't want charity.'"

Coun. McQuire went on to say that the average earnings of many families was only 26s per week. How could a man, his wife and a large family be supported on that sum? No assistance could be looked for from the Prince of Wales' Fund because, prior to the new concessions, relief was not given to anyone earning more than 24s per week. "It was a scandal," said the Councillor, bitterly, "When the Prince of Wales' fund was raised we subscribed liberally, and, until now, relief has been refused to us in our extremity.'"

The strike had spread to Fatfield School. On 19 November 1917, '25 of our boys absented themselves yesterday afternoon and 7 this morning in sympathy with the strike instigated at Washington and Usworth by the men to enforce the feeding of necessitous schoolchildren.' So it was at Glebe School where the Headmaster, although not convinced that all absence was as a result of the strike, noted in his Log that attendance was down but that, 'there has been no picketing in connection with the affair and I can hear of no act of violence against the children attending'. He added, 'Usworth schools have been more affected than the Washington ones but mining is practically the only employment there in Usworth, while we have the Chemical Works and Cook's ironworks in Washington.' [Cook's ironworks was indeed an employer but it was having problems, like the pits. See below.]

Children were expected to do their bit for food supplies. An entry in Fatfield Council School's Log Book for July 1915 reads, 'The children have taken up with enthusiasm the idea of collecting fresh eggs for the wounded soldiers in hospital, in connection with the National Egg Collection, and this week we have dispatched 190 fresh eggs to headquarters.' And that was not to be all. In March 1916 the Log noted, 'In view of the shortage of food in the country due to the

Great War, the Education Committee have secured from the Lambton Estate a Plot of Ground opposite the Boys' play-ground to be used in the production of food in connection with School Gardening now being introduced as a special subject.

'The Plot is 2 chains long by 1 chain wide or 968 square yards and is to be fenced around. The Plot will be worked as opportunity and weather permit.

'70 of the most suitable and capable boys are registered in 5 classes of 14 each, 2 under Mr Stables, 2 under Mr Peebles and one with myself.'

In 1918 the school started sending the children out blackberrying. Thus, 27 September, 'Standards VII and VI went to black-berrying again this afternoon in charge of Mr Stables and Mr Peebles and the registers were not marked according to the Education Committee's arrangement. 59 lbs were forwarded.' On 1 October, 'Same as before, 39 lbs were gathered.' 3 October, 'Stds VII and VI were out again this afternoon, gathering blackberries under the care of Mr Stables, over 70 lbs being collected. 201 lbs of berries have been sent in altogether.' [Usworth Council Mixed School collected 129 lbs in October 1918 and the Headmaster noted that this was, 'as directed by the Food Controller'.]

J.W.Cook's

The Chester-le-Street Chronicle in July 1917 reported on the Annual General Meeting of Joseph Cook, Sons and Co Ltd, 'During the year ending 30/9/16 there was a very reduced demand for coal tubs and colliery work generally and having regards to this fact, and that a considerable number of the workmen joined the colours during the period in question, it was found impossible to secure labour owing to the war.' [The St George's, Harraton, Roll of Honour lists eighteen men from Cook's, of whom seven were killed – **Alfred Braban, Richard Drummond, Robert S Gould, Stephen Mills, John F Potter, Charles Smith** and **George B Smith.** There were many other employees who lived in other parts of Washington.] Several factors were offered as the reason why profits had fallen to £626.12.11. At an earlier meeting of the directors, 6 July, note was made that the company had been compelled to considerably increase the wages of their workmen but some consolation was evident in that, 'by production of shells and other war material we have been able to contribute in some way to the requirements of H.M. Government during the present war'.

At the same meeting of directors it was moved, by the Chairman, that the salary of J. Falshaw Cook, as Managing Director, should be increased from 1 October 1915 to 30 September 1916 from £360 p.a. to £500 p.a. and from 1 October 1916 from £500 p.a. to £900 p.a. and that the salary of Joseph Cook, as Director, be increased from 1 October 1916 from £312 p.a. to £900 p.a. [Profits down, salaries up, who says history does not repeat itself?]

The firm of Joseph Cook and Sons Ltd had been established in 1900 out of Washington Iron Works, which had been started by C. and J. Cook sometime prior to 1860. It was an iron and steel foundry and, as we shall see, many other things as well. Based at Washington Station, it remained a family business, with James Falshaw Cook Jr. being appointed Joint Managing Director in 1925.

The stated aims of the firm were to, 'carry on all or any of the trades or businesses of Iron Masters, Iron Merchants, Iron Manufacturers, Steel Manufacturers, Metal Founders, Workers and Converters, Colliery Owners, Miners and Smelters, Engine Builders, Boilermakers, Waggon Builders, Mining Tub, Corv and Truck Builders, Mechanical and Electrical, Heat, Motor Power, Water Supply and Sanitary and General Engineers, Manufacturers of Agricultural Implements and other Machinery, Tool Makers, Fitters, Electroplaters, Millwrights, Ironmongers, Builders, Carpenters and Joiners, Woodworkers, Box and Packing Case Manufacturers, Painters, Metallurgists, Gas Manufacturers, Farmers, Printers, Shipowners, Shipbuilders, Charterers of Vessels, Carriers by Sea and Land, Wharfingers, Deckowners, Warehousemen and to buy, sell, manufacture, repair, convert, alter, let on hire and deal in machinery, implements, rolling stock and hardware of all kinds.'

The Illustrated Chronicle reported the death of Mr J. Cook in March 1915.

'WASHINGTON IRONMASTER'S DEATH

The death is reported at his residence, Cumberland House, Harrogate, of Mr Joseph Cook in his 70th year. Mr Cook, who led an active business life up to within a few days of his death, was managing director of the firm of Joseph Cook Sons & Co Ltd, Washington Iron Works, County Durham and until recently lived at North Biddick Hall, Washington and Keldy Castle, Pickering, Yorkshire.

He was a magistrate for the County of Durham and, for a number of years, held a commission in the 4th Volunteer Brigade, DLI, retiring with the rank of Lt Colonel, receiving the Volunteer Officers' Decoration. Mr Cook leaves a widow, three sons and five daughters.'

Casualties

The Washington Holy Trinity Church Parish magazine for May 1917 noted, 'Pro Patria – **Thomas Penaluna, John Tatters** and **James Patterson**. Our very real sympathy goes out to those who mourn the above. Mrs Patterson, one of our most devoted Churchworkers has lost a son. We wish particularly to her the feeling and sympathy of our Church people. May God grant her and all those who mourn His Presence and Peace to console and comfort them at this time.' These words may well have been composed by Reverend Cyril Lomax, who was absent from his parish duties, acting as a chaplain in France.

The first of the, approximately ninety-six, Washington soldiers and sailors to die in 1917 was **Thomas Nattrass.** The Battalion War Diary of 6 East Yorkshires indicates that they were near Engelbelmer, near Albert, at the end of 1916, working on completing trenches, laying duck-board track and repairing dug-outs, work that was going on day and night. The diary states that 'work continued on 1 January', but makes no mention of any casualties suffered, 'nothing to report'. A letter, from Lieutenant W.R. Coles, was received by Mrs Nattrass,

Thomas Nattrass plaque.
(Family)

'Dear Madam, I feel I must write to offer you my most sincere sympathy on the death of your husband. I always found him so willing to assist in any work however hard or disagreeable. He was killed by a shell as he was returning from work and both his mules were killed under him. In the

Thomas Nattrass. (Family)

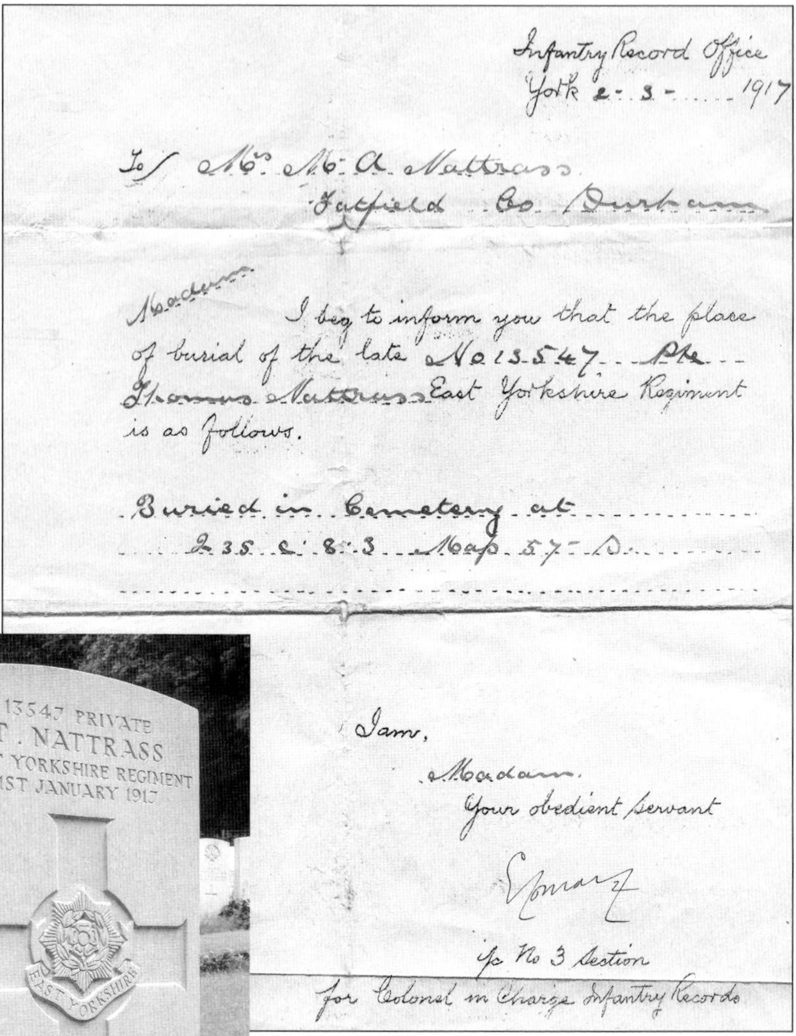

Handwritten letter:

Infantry Record Office
York 2-3-....1917

To/ Mrs. M. A. Nattrass.
Fatfield Co. Durham

Madam,
        I beg to inform you that the place
of burial of the late No 13547 Pte
Thomas Nattrass East Yorkshire Regiment
is as follows.

Buried in Cemetery at
235.c.8.3. Map.57.D.

I am,
    Madam,
        Your obedient Servant

        Thomas?

        i/c No 3 Section
for Colonel in Charge Infantry Records

Thomas Nattrass – information re location of his grave. (Family)

Thomas Nattrass grave in Aveluy Wood. (Family)

The Landing at Suvala Bay

You may talk of Balaclava
And of Trafalga Bay
But what about the 11th Division
Who landed at Suvala Bay

They were part of Kitchener's Army
Some had left children and Wifes
But they fought for Englands Freedom
Fought for there very lifes

It was on the 6th of August
When they made the terrible dash
And the Turks on the hillside
Our boats were trying to smash

The order came fix Bayonets
So out of the boats they got
Every man there was an hero
Who was facing that Hellish lot

Funnels of ships were smashed
While the sea in some parts was red
But they fought there way through the ocean
To the beach that was covered with dead

Creeping at last up the Hillside
While shot and shell fell around
They made a last desperate effort
And charged the Turkish ground

The Turks at last gave up
When they saw the bayonets play
So they turned there backs on the British
And retired from Suvala Bay

There was the Lincolns, Dorsetts, and Staffords
And Notts and Derbys too
The Borders Reg were there
A rough and angry crew.

Then we got the Manchesters
With the Lancs Fusiliers by there side
The Boys that come from Lancashire
Will fill our hearts with pride

There was the Yorks, the East Yorks and West Yorks
The Yorks and Lancs as well
Who fought for good old Yorkshire
Were among the lads that fell

The fighting fifth were fighting hard
Northumberland lads you know
While the Duke of Wellingtons
Were keeping back the foe

And far away on the Hillside
Lying beneath the clay
Are some of the lads who died
While trying to win the day

So remember the 11th Division
Who were all Volunteers you know
But they fought and died like Heroes
While going to face the foe

Thomas Nattrass poem about landing at Suvla Bay. (Family)

death of your husband I feel I have lost not only a very able and valuable man but also a personal friend, he had been under me so long. There will be many out here who mourn his death as deeply as I do and who will sympathise with you in your great sorrow. Yours faithfully.'

Robert Stephenson Gould, who served in the Grimsby Chums [10 Lincolnshire], was listed missing in April 1917 but is believed to have been one of twenty British soldiers discovered in a mass grave in 2001. Without recourse to DNA testing, his body remains 'unknown' but was one of the twenty re-buried in Point du Jour Cemetery, near Arras.

Robert Stephenson Gould. (Family)

R.S.Gould at Point du Jour Cemetery. (Author)

R.S.Gould on Arras Memorial. (Author)

Leonard Sidney Claudian Davison may sound like the name of an officer but he was a mere lance corporal when killed near Polygon Wood in October 1917. His brother, **Henderson Richardson Davison**, was killed in October 1918. Brothers Cecil Theodore, Norman and George also served. Their sisters were Irene Vesta Ophelia and Ena Jessie Olga. The Davisons liked distinctive names. The family lived at the delightfully named Girdle Cake Cottage.

Davison family. (Family)

Girdle Cake Cottage. (Beamish Museum)

James O'Neill's scroll and tube. (Family)

BUCKINGHAM PALACE.

I join with my grateful people
in sending you this memorial
of a brave life given for others
in the Great War.

George R.I.

James O'Neill's grave. (Family)

James O'Neill's grave in St Joseph's churchyard, Birtley. (Author)

James O'Neill was home on leave when killed by a bus on Durham Road in 1917. He had gone to the Barley Mow pub with his father-in-law and, when a bus approached them from behind, they panicked, stepped in front of it and sustained fatal injuries. **James** had three brothers killed in France and his cousin, **Patrick Murphy**, was killed while serving in the RAF. The inquest into the road fatalities placed no blame on the driver, a Belgian ex-soldier.

John Whittaker claimed to have been born in Kurri Kurri, New South Wales when he joined the Australian Army – though it seems as if he was probably born in Usworth. He was killed in October 1917. **John's** effects were sent to his father on 16 October 1917 and consisted of a wallet, testament, fountain pen, disc, handkerchief and photographs. His father also received his plaque, in September 1922, and a pamphlet entitled 'Where the Australians Rest'. **John's** will, dated 20 June 1917, had stated that he left £10 to Mrs G. McMahon and £10 to Mrs J McMahon of Felling and the rest was to go to his father.

James O'Neill. (Illustrated Chronicle)

   The year ended with a small party for the Glebe School children. The Headmaster noted in his Log in early January 1918, 'On Christmas Eve 183 scholars of the three departments [infants, juniors and mixed] who are children of soldiers or widows were entertained to tea and an apple was given to each on leaving.' Earlier in the year, on 13 April 1917, *The Chester-le-Street Chronicle* reported that 900 'Jack and Tommy's bairns' were entertained at the Empire in Chester-le-Street. Each of them was given a greeting card from the king and kueen and a box of toffees. Fifty-two children whose fathers had been killed were given the toffees and a bible, suitably inscribed. The money for the gifts had been raised at weekly dances.

CHAPTER 9

1918 ... Summary: Profiteering, Potatoes, Fish, Casualties

1918 was the last year of the war but on 1 January there would have been few who could have imagined that would be the case. A Bruce Bairnsfather cartoon, dated by him 'A.D 1950', shows Old Bill and Bert, now bearded Methuselahs, watching the shells flying over their heads while the pair discuss the arrival of the War Babies Battalion. Point made. American doughboys were on their way, but so were a large number of German divisions, released from the Eastern Front by the collapse of Russia. The French were not exactly stable and Douglas Haig was short of troops as a result of Lloyd George's reluctance to send more troops to his command. In the spring and early summer the Allies found themselves retreating westwards and it was not until August that the tide really turned and the Allies began the advance that would lead to the German request for an Armistice.

Profiteering

With food in such short supply there were concerns about, and restrictions on, 'profiteering'. *The Chester-le-Street Chronicle* of 18 June 1918 reported that, 'John Scott, 69, Fatfield, was summoned for having sold nut toffee at 2½d per ounce, instead of 2d, and clear gums at 3d per ounce instead of 2d per ounce as fixed by the Sugar

(Confectionary) Order, on 6 April and Annie Bridges, his daughter, was summoned for having acted as his agent in the two transactions.

'Scott appeared and pleaded guilty on the first charge on behalf of himself and his daughter, who did not appear, but not guilty on the other charges.

'Mr J. Hargreaves prosecuted and said that the Order had been in force over twelve months. Though they had taken out summonses in two cases they had only asked for a conviction in one.

'Mark Williams, Long Row, Fatfield said he went to the shop and asked for quarter pound of nut toffee, quarter pound of clear gums and one ounce of jubes. He handed over half a crown and only received 6d change and on being questioned Mrs Bridges said the price of his toffee was 2½d per ounce and the clear gums 3d. He asked if this was not too much but she replied "no". He said he would complain and she replied that he could do as he pleased. He complained to the Chester-le-Street Rural Food Control Committee.

'Inspector T.S. Wadge said he was instructed to make enquiries and, on going to the shop with Wilkinson he was informed by the defendant Bridges that she did not know sweets were controlled. She had raised the price because the retailers had increased the price to her.'Mr Hargreaves said there had been numerous complaints about the same thing from that district.

'Scott was fined 40s in the first case and 10s in the second; and Bridges was fined 10s and 5s; and 7s witnesses' expenses in addition.

'Mr Hargreaves said at the price charged the profit was 8/8d on a 4 lb box.'

Others to appear in court on food-related offences were Henry Sharp (18) and his accomplice, George Cumpson (16). They appeared before magistrates in October 1917 charged with the theft of apples from the orchard of William Hall. The type and number of apples were not detailed but the miscreants were fined twenty-five shillings each. Wow, that would make a hole in family budgets. That Dora, she had teeth.

Potatoes

In March 1915 Barmston Parish Council received a letter and some leaflets from the Ministry of Agriculture and Fisheries, the leaflets outlining how potatoes should be grown by allotment-holders and gardeners.

Then, in January 1917, Durham County War Agriculture Committee offered seed potatoes to allotment holders and small cultivators and Barmston and Washington council agreed to canvas the area to see who wished to participate. The potatoes would be 2s per stone and, the potatoes having been delivered to Washington station, the councillors agreed to do the work of distribution and money collection. However, there was concern that the potatoes had not been delivered by the April meeting.

In April 1918 *The Chester-le-Street Chronicle* carried a piece in which it was pointed out that in 1917 County Durham had produced 61,000 tons of potatoes and that the people of County Durham had consumed 133,900 tons of potatoes, leaving a deficit of 72,900 tons.

Lord Rhondda, Minister of Food Control, and Mr Prothero [perhaps the Potato Tsar of the Ministry], stated the paper, 'appeal to every man who has a farm, a garden or an allotment to plant more potatoes and make the county self-supporting'.

Fish – the lack of

In June 1917, under a heading, **'THE FISHLESS WEAR'**, *The Chester-le-Street Chronicle* reported on the sending of a petition to the Secretary of the Freshwater Fish Committee of the government about the lack of fish in the Wear from above Durham to Sunderland. Apparently the river had been well stocked with eels, trout and coarse fish but pollution had caused them to disappear. Some polluters, not named, had been fined but that money had not been used to re-stock the river and 'we consider that, from a food supply point of view, such a state of things should not be allowed to exist'. The Wear Fishery Board had agreed to seek statutory power to prevent pollution by product works and the local anglers were strongly in favour of that.

The Secretary of the Petition Committee received a prompt supply from the secretary, Hon. A.S. Northcote, in which the latter recognized the gravity of the subject and said that his committee would investigate closely 'with a view to ascertaining what can be done to ameliorate matters'. The paper then quoted Mr Craggs from Houghton-le-Spring, who reminisced in great detail about the fishing in days gone by – how one man caught 250 flatfish, how flatfish could be picked up by the handful at Fatfield, how the old fishermen sat on the low jetty at Fatfield and how there were shoals of fish at Chatershaugh and Lambton Park. On one occasion a gentleman stopped and congratulated him on his catch and it turned out to be no other than Lord Scarborough!

Casualties

John Frederick Potter MM and Bar, was born at Chester-le-Street, enlisted at Shiney Row on 22 September 1914 and was resident at West Bridge Street. He served as Lance Corporal 20715, 15 DLI, and was

J.F. Potter letter to Mrs Armstrong.
(Jim Foster)

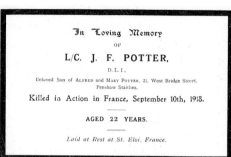

To freedom's cause his life he gave
And dared the battle purpose sure
A hero write upon his grave,
He died that England might endure

" THY WILL BE DONE."

W Clarke & Son, Ltd., Chester-le-Street.

In Loving Memory

OF

L/C. J. F. POTTER,

D. L. I,

Beloved Son of ALFRED and MARY POTTER, 21, West Bridge Street,
Penshaw Staithes,

Killed in Action in France, September 10th, 1918.

AGED 22 YEARS.

Laid at Rest at St. Eloi, France.

J.F.Potter In Memoriam card. (Jim Foster)

killed on 10 September 1918. At the time of his enlistment **John Frederick** was nineteen years old, a labourer. Though he won the MM and Bar, his service record was not unblemished. In October 1915 he was awaiting trial for 'using threatening language to his superior officer' and was sentenced to six months Field Punishment No 1, sentence commuted to three months FP No 1 by a brigadier general in November. He was also deprived of his stripe, for misconduct, in December 1917.

'News has come to hand of the death in action of **Lance Corporal John F Potter** (22), DLI, MM of Penshaw Staithes, and late of Fatfield, who made the supreme sacrifice on September 10th. This valiant young soldier had been out in France about three years having enlisted at the outbreak of war. He had taken part in many engagements and had been gassed. In August 1917 he won the MM through conspicuous bravery in the field, having with the aid of about four or five comrades kept the machine gun going until help arrived and thus saved the situation. Just one year after this meritorious recognition he added further lustre to his name and gained the recognition of his Commanding Officer for which a Bar was added to his MM. The people of Fatfield were contemplating presenting him with a gold watch on his homecoming but this will now be handed to his nearest relative. Previous to joining up, this brave soldier was in the employ of the Harraton Colliery and the Iron Works Co at Bewicke Main. A brother of the deceased, **Pte Alfred H Potter**, was also killed in action – on 4th August, 1916. They were the only two sons of a family of eight children.'

Thomas Scorer, one of six children, was born on 7 April 1894 at New Lambton. He joined the Navy in May 1918 for the length of hostilities (the army called it 'for the duration') and served, or was trained, on HMS *Victory II* until May, at which point he became Stoker 2nd Class K/51313 on HMS *Glatton*. After his death, on 16 September 1918, from injuries sustained in the explosion described below, he was buried in Gillingham Woodlands Cemetery. **Thomas** left a widow, Mary Ellen, nee Lindsey, [she had already been widowed when **Herbert Lindsay** was killed in 1916], living at 13 Oxclose St, Washington. They had married at Holy Trinity Church, Washington as recently as 16 July 1918. Elizabeth Scorer, their daughter, was baptized in March 1919, her father described as 'deceased' and a 'stoker in the Royal Navy'. Mrs Scorer received a war gratuity but the amount is not stated in **Thomas'** record.

HMS *Glatton* joined the Dover Patrol on 11 September 1918, and lay in harbour ready to depart for the Belgian coast. On 16 September the ship suddenly, and without warning, blew up and began burning furiously. The forward magazines were flooded, but due to the flames her aft magazines could not be, and thus the risk of further explosion was imminent. More importantly, the ship in the next berth was a fully-loaded ammunition ship: if HMS *Glatton* blew up, the ammunition ship would explode also, threatening to seriously damage the town of Dover and causing thousands of civilian casualties. Three torpedoes were fired into her hull and *Glatton* rolled over and sank; sixty of her crew of 305 officers and men were missing, and 124 injured, nineteen of whom later died of burns.

George Hedley Ainsley attested at Houghton-le-Spring in October 1916 and was placed into Army Reserve Class B. He was seventeen, a putter, and living at 4 High Chapel Row. When examined in April 1918 he was five feet four inches tall, weighed 119 lbs and was described as having a fresh complexion, light brown hair and brown eyes.

George Hedley Ainsley.
(Family)

He had a birthmark below his right clavicle and a mole below his left groin. His physical development was described as 'good'. **Hedley**, as the family knew him, was born at Birtley.

George Hedley was posted to 12 Battalion DLI in August 1918 and died of wounds in 29 Casualty Clearing Station, Italy, on 30 October 1918. His death was announced in *The Chester-le-Street Chronicle* in the edition of 6 December 1918 – 'Eldest son of Mr and Mrs John Ainsley of Fatfield –

"With aching hearts we shook his hand
Tears glistened in our eye
We wished him luck but little thought
It was our last goodbye."'

The family received their son's War Medal and the Victory Medal in April 1919. In July 1919 they received a letter from the Infantry Record Office at York telling them that it had been necessary to exhume their son's body [it does not say from where] so that it could be reburied, 'with all due care and reverence by an army chaplain', in Giavera Cemetery. Standing at his grave, in an olive grove in the foothills above Venice, the campanile tower of St Mark's can be seen. Though it was not mentioned in his record, **George Hedley's** possessions must have been sent home

G.H.Ainsley grave at Giavera Cemetery. (Author)

because a coin, perhaps Egyptian, which had been carried by him, was given to his brother, John, and the latter's name was stamped into the coin. He carried it through the Second World War on HMS *Dido* and it was then left to John's son, George Hedley, now an elderly gentleman,

G.H.Ainsley coin.(Family)

still living in Harraton. The present George Hedley has a memory of being told that his uncle was killed by a sniper's bullet and can remember his grandmother crying at the kitchen table years after the event.

Patrick Murphy was born in 1896 in Washington. In the 1911 Census he was living with his parents, Michael and Ellen, and seven siblings, at 47 Havannah Terrace.

The Roman Catholic Memorial lists **Sergeant P Murphy** as being killed in action on 15 May 1918, aged twenty five. This information

Patrick Murphy – seated. (Family)

fits with the Absent Voters List of 1918, which included **Patrick Murphy** of 47, Havannah Terrace, serving as '61926, 2nd AM Royal Air Force'. The CWGC states that **Sergeant Murphy** was serving in 48 Squadron and was an observer. He is commemorated on the Arras Flying Services Memorial.

Arras Memorial to RAF/RFC. (Author)

A postcard, dated 11 May 18, four days before he was killed, from **Patrick** to his father at 47 Havannah Terrace, reads, 'Dear Mother and Father, Just a line to let you know that I sail for France tomorrow afternoon, and will write you a line when I get to my destination. I have been made a sargent [sic] observer, so cheers and keep a good heart. Goodnight from **Pat**. Xxxxxx.' The photograph was of The Bank and Royal Exchange, London.

Another postcard, not dated, was sent to Mr Murphy at 47 Havannah Terrace and reads, 'Dear Father, Just a line hoping you are in good health as I am at present. I am sorry that I couldn't send any more fancy cards just yet, but I will get some next time I get paid. Wishing you a merry Xmas and a Happy New Year. From **Pat**.' The card showed the organ staircase at Rouen's l'Église Saint Maclou.

 Patrick Murphy is listed on the Memorial to the men of F Pit, Washington, the Catholic Memorial and the Washington Memorial.

Sarah Ferguson is the only woman named on the Washington War Memorial. In the 1901 census the family were at 56 Wagonman's Row. **Sarah** was one year old.

James and Mary Ferguson, married since 1899, were living in Havannah Terrace [no number given] in 1911, with their six surviving children. **Sarah** had five sisters and a brother. Mr Ferguson Sr., a widower, was living with them. James was a bank labourer. The death certificate for **Sarah Ferguson** states that she died at 61 Havannah Terrace on 23 June 1918. Her father, James, was present at her death, the cause of which was phthisis pulmonares, i.e. tuberculosis. Her death was certified by Dr William Jacques.

Speculation in **Sarah's** family is that she was a nursing assistant, perhaps at Blackfell Sanatorium, which was not far away from Havannah Terrace.

The Roll of Honour drawn up for Washington and Barmston Parishes included **Sarah Ferguson** but gave no address.

Frederick Armstrong was born in Newbottle in 1889 and was a married coal miner when he attested on 4 November 1914. He was five feet four inches tall, weighed 124 lbs, and was sallow-complexioned, with brown hair and eyes. He became Private 14796, 1/4th East Yorkshire Regiment. He was married to Ethel (née Moon) and their children – Mary Ann, Elizabeth G and Frederick A – were born in, respectively, 1904, 1912 and 1916. A current family member states that

Fred Archer Armstrong (i.e. Fred Jr.) was named after Fred Archer, champion jockey from 1874–1886 and rider of twenty-six classic winners, including the Derby on five occasions. Mary Ann [Polly] bore Bryan Ferry of Roxy Music.

Fred was sent to Egypt in September 1915 and, while in the Mediterranean Expeditionary Force, spent some time in hospital in Malta, suffering from scabies. He returned to the Western Front on 3 July 1916 and was posted missing 'on or since 25 April 1918'. **Fred** is commemorated on the Tyne Cot Memorial. His name also appears on the plaque in Beverley Minster to the men of the East Yorkshire Regiment.

Ethel and her children were awarded a pension of 29/7d per week from 23 December 1918 and received the medals to which **Fred's** service had entitled him – the War, and Victory medals and the 1915 Star.

Fred Armstrong. (Family)

CHAPTER 10

The Brave Men Living and Dead ...

In March 1915 news came that Corporal Mulvey of Fatfield, 2nd Leinster Regiment, had won the Distinguished Conduct Medal. Patrick Mulvey had joined the army at eighteen, in 1898, served in Canada, the West Indies and the South African campaign and was in the Army Reserve when war broke out. He was recalled to the colours and served in France from 9 September 1914 until he was discharged from the army in September 1915. By that time he had been shot in the face, right arm and leg. Details of the citation (*London Gazette*, 1 April 1915) for his DCM were as follows: 'For conspicuous gallantry, ability and coolness after every officer and non-commissioned officer had been put out of action in a German assault he assumed command and with great determination directed effective fire on the enemy and kept his own men well in hand.' The incident occurred on 1 May 1915 at Premésques, a village between Loos and Armentières.

Washington Parish Council meeting of October 1915 noted that a public meeting had been called for 7 pm Thursday, 18 October, to recognize service of Sapper C.M. Collette, who was awarded the DCM for bravery in France.

In January 1916, 'Lance Corporal Charles Collette DCM of Washington Station was accorded a public reception and presentation of War Script by the parishioners of Washington in the National School, Washington, on Thursday night. Lance Corporal Collette, who belongs to the Royal Engineers, was one of the successful company who mined some German trenches and, through coolness and bravery, maintained the position.' His DCM citation in the *London Gazette* on 9 October 1915 reads, '82622 Sapper C.M. Collette, 173rd Tunnelling Co. For conspicuous bravery and decision when engaged, with another man, in pushing forward advanced galleries through those of the enemy, thereby determining the success of the mining operations. Any loss of coolness and presence of mind would have led to the discovery and loss of the advanced workings, and possibly also to the destruction of the whole of the galleries.'

Lance Corporal E.W. Chicken, 10th DLI, was awarded the DCM, 'For conspicuous gallantry. Lance Corporal Chicken, on two occasions, went out to within seventy yards of the enemy trenches, and carried in wounded men, exhibiting great bravery and devotion to duty (*London Gazette,* 11 March 1916).'

15667 Sergeant W. Simpson won his DCM, 'For conspicuous gallantry and devotion to duty during a successful daylight raid. He outflanked and rushed an enemy bombing post, killing and capturing the garrison, and by his dash and courage setting a fine example to his men. The success of his enterprise very materially added to the success of the whole raid.' (L.G. 25 August 1917.) He had earlier been awarded the MM and, according to *The Illustrated Chronicle*, had a bar added to that.

Having gone to France on 13 July 1915, **George Brabben Smith** participated, and was killed, in the attack on Fricourt on 1 July 1916. **Lance Corporal Smith's** citation for his DCM reads as follows: 'For conspicuous gallantry when in charge of a bombing party during a counterattack he held his position under heavy fire for one hour after being wounded, refusing to leave and have his wound dressed. He built a barricade across the communications trench leading towards the enemy.'

A presentation to three Washington soldiers was reported in January 1916. 'Company **Sergeant Major Claughan**, Corporal James Watson and Private John Hanlon, all members of Washington Station Westwood Club, being back on leave from the front, the members subscribed amongst themselves sufficient to purchase each a luminous wristlet watch. Mr D. McBirnie presided at the gathering and the presentations were made by Mr William Tempest.'

Harraton Parish organized at least four presentations to those who had been decorated. *The Chester-le-Street Chronicle* covered the first of the ceremonies, in June 1917, as follows:

'HONOURING THE BRAVE
PRESENTATION AT FATFIELD BY LORD DURHAM
40 SOLDIERS KILLED

Considerable interest was evinced and enthusiasm displayed at Fatfield on Saturday afternoon at the presentation of a gold wristlet watch to Capt. G.S. Nelson by the Rt. Hon the Earl of Durham K.G., who was accompanied by Lady Anne Lambton. The whole village was *en fete* and the Shiney Row Brass Band paraded the main street. The weather being fine, the proceedings were held in the open-air, an emergency platform being provided in the shape of a dray. Mr James Wilson and Mrs Walton, respectively chairman and clerk to Harraton Parish Council, were responsible for the arrangements.

'The hero of the day is the only son of Mr and Mrs W. Nelson, Nova Scotia. He enlisted as a despatch rider and was soon recommended for a commission. Going to the front as a second lieutenant in one of the new battalions of the Northumberland Fusiliers, he was promoted full lieutenant for good work. He took part in the strenuous work of the first day of the Somme Push, where occurred this opportunity, which he grasped, of obtaining distinction. He was nine months in France without receiving a scratch but on July 1st a bullet struck him which happily entered his pocket book and was deflected from its course.

'In the absence of Mr Donkin, the Vicar of Fatfield, Rev. Reeman, presided. In his introductory remarks he said he was pleased to see such a large gathering present to do honour to Captain Nelson. At the same time he was a representative of all the boys and they should think of them all. It was especially fitting to do so at this time when they had secured the greatest victory in the present war (VIMY RIDGE). The glorious peace that they anticipated so confidently would be due to the strenuous efforts of their soldiers, sailors and airmen. (Applause.) Fatfield had nobly responded to the call of duty. 400

men had gone from that village and, he was sad to say, though it was a glorious thing, 40 had made the supreme sacrifice. [In fact 57 had been killed by the end of June 1917] They had no need to tell the people there to be abstemious; they had to be when the collieries were working so badly. At the end of the war they proposed to have a memorial to those who had laid down their lives. There were also watches to present to Corporal L.C. Robinson and Private G. Mossman when the opportunity arose. He was glad they had Captain Nelson, who had been through several severe engagements, in their midst that day.

'A collection was then taken in aid of the fund.

'Lord Durham added further praise for Captain Nelson and remarked that England, and now America, would never give up until liberty and freedom had been gained for the world.

'Capt G.S. Nelson, who received a great ovation, said he looked upon the presentation as a great honour and he much appreciated it. He would sooner be back in the trenches than facing the audience. The majority of men he had with him were from Durham and Northumberland and there were no finer fighters in the world. The first battalion he was with included men he had known all his life and what were left were still going strong.

'Mr G.W. Minto, in proposing a vote of thanks to his Lordship; said he hoped he would be with them at their next presentation. Mr James Wilson briefly seconded. The singing of the National Anthem terminated proceedings.'

A month later Gunner George Mossman of Castle Street was presented by Mr Minto, manager of Harraton Colliery, with a gold wristlet watch suitably inscribed. After a procession from Gunner Mossman's home, some patriotic remarks were made by Mr John Donkin to the assembled crowd and he noted that, 'There appeared to have got afloat an impression that the committee, which was arranging these presentations, proposed to make distinctions or fish of one and flesh of another. This was not so. Every man, whoever he was and whatever his rank, if he lived in the parish of Harraton, would receive the same consideration and a similar presentation would be made to him.'

'Mr Donkin stated that, 'there was a certain and sure victory coming to England and her Allies. (Applause.) They could not tell when it would come but so long as they knew it was coming it was all right. The Russian revolution and the entry of America had altered the whole current of the war. In the days that were to come the people at home must stand solidly and true to the lads who had fought so bravely and well on the battlefield. They might have a severe struggle before them but what could any sacrifices be, by those who remained at home, compared to those that the soldiers made at the front. He was sure they would stand by the lads until they marched home again with the flags of victory flying.

'Mr Minto said he was glad to be the one chosen to make that presentation to one of their own lads,' and added that, 'He had that morning seen one of his sons back to the front. He was known as the Pitman Officer and he said that the Durham miners were held in high esteem as soldiers by officers and men at the front. (Applause)'. [Mr Minto did not mention that his other son, Lt Oswald Minto, had been court-martialled for drunkenness, though he went on to serve as a private in a different regiment.]

Gunner Mossman said he had, 'pleasure in thanking them for the kind manner in which they had received him and for that very handsome presentation that they had made to him. He hoped it would not be long before they marched home after victory and a prolonged peace for the old country. (Loud applause.)'

In October 1917, 'There was a large attendance at the Co-operative Hall, Fatfield, on Saturday night when a series of presentations were made to the mothers of soldiers and ambulance men. Mr J. Kelly, North Biddick, presided, and the presentations were made by Mr A. Kirkup, agent for the Lambton and Hetton Collieries Co, by whom practically all the men are employed.

'During the evening a musical entertainment was given by the Misses Cumpson, May and Joyce, Mrs Crozier and Messrs C. Stables, W. Bohill and Rogerson, Mr Finlay's company and the Fatfield Welcome Home Band whilst Mrs Stables accompanied on the piano.

'Mr Kirkup said it was a peculiarly good thing that the people of Durham should take steps to recognize the lads who had won recognition on the field. If the lads who had won these medals could have been present that night they would probably have agreed that there were thousands of men who deserved Victoria Crosses but never got them'. He went on to praise the heroism of **William Moore** and **John G Charlton** and said it was a terrible thing that neither lad had been spared to return to their families but perhaps it would be some consolation to know that their sons had been recognized by their officers and their own village.

A very similar occasion took place in the Co-operative Hall in September 1918, at which Mr Kirkup, agent for Lambton and Hetton Collieries, said, 'No parish in the district has done better than Harraton and Fatfield. There was a population of a little over 3,000 in the village and of this number 700 men had joined the forces – one in every five of the population. Seventy of these had laid down their lives, that was one in every ten of those who went out and twelve had won distinctions. They were making presentations to three of their brave men of the parish.' (In fact the St George's Roll of Honour lists 410 men who served and 102 are known to have died.)

Gunner Mossman was awarded his Military Medal, Captain R.C. Thomas, manager of North Biddick Colliery, was presented with a gold watch for being awarded the Military Cross and Sergeant J.F. Seagar was presented with a gold watch for being awarded the Belgian Croix de Guerre.

In April 1919 *The Chester-le-Street Chronicle* reported, 'At an Investiture held at Buckingham Palace on Saturday last, Lieutenant Robert A. Dent, late of 10th Northumberland Fusiliers, was decorated by His Majesty the King with the Military Cross for the following conspicuous act of gallantry during the severe fighting near the Menin Road in Sept 1917 –

"In an advance he reached his objective with only three men but held it till reinforcements arrived. He also captured a field gun after a hard struggle."'

CHAPTER 11

For Us the War Is Over

In October 1918 the Head Teacher of Biddick Council Infants noted, 'Many absences due to sickness. Miss Winter also ill on Thursday because of influenza, to reopen October 28th.' And later, 'Received further notice to remain closed until 18th November.' Then, on November 20th, 'Reopened on 18th November. Poor attendance. Received notice on Tuesday to close until 29th November.' Then, in January 1919, 'Reopened Tuesday after closure for epidemic and Christmas holidays.' Owing to the influenza epidemic the school was open only seven full weeks from midsummer to Christmas. Thus it was that Washington schools' log books made no reference to the end of the war.

The quarterly report of Chester-le-Street Co-op in January 1919 included, 'Our first thought is one of joy and pleasure.....that the comparative peace and tranquillity reigns in our land. The great guns are silent and the perils and anxieties of aircraft invasion are a thing of the past.'

We have no record of events in Washington itself but, as *The Chester-le-Street Chronicle* headlined it,

'THE END OF THE WAR - TIDINGS OF PEACE
How they were received locally
GREAT REJOICINGS
Chester-le-Street's pent-up joy broke loose on Monday morning shortly after eleven o'clock, when official news was received that the armistice had been signed and that we had seen

Peace celebrations in Washington.

the end of the Great World War. There was a quick run on flags of all descriptions, which speedily made their appearance from every street corner and window until the whole town was beflagged. The tiny tot had its own miniature Union Jack while the more majestic Royal Standard and other national emblems were seen furling in the breeze. Streamers were run across the Front Street at various points and everyone was fraternizing with each other upon the glorious news received.

'But the celebration did not partake in any way of Mafeking, though everyone rejoiced and felt that life would have again its true purpose for them in a new and better world. Many were sad at heart at the loss of loved ones whom they mourned by reason of the cruel war and the news, although joyful in the extreme, for the moment forced the doors of memory back and vacant chairs appeared vivid to them. They realized as they had never done before how sad and solemn even was the joyful news.'

The paper described the day as one of nature's grandest and remarked that the word was spread by 'buzzers, sirens and every kind of medium that was available'. Bells rang out in all parishes and a *feu-de-joie* was fired. Bells 'rang out a gladsome clarion, such sweet music

as appealed to all as never before, as many of the bells had hung
listlessly and silently for four years in their high belfries.

'At noon many ceased work.... the buses stopped running as the
girls voted themselves a half-holiday, while during the evening
the buzzers from the pits issued forth their well-known signal
that the pits would be idle next day. The relaxation of the
Lighting Order both as to the shop windows and the street lamps
gave everyone a realization of pre-war times again and how the
crowd revelled in it.

'At dusk the streets were incommodiously crowded with a
crowd of irrepressible and irresponsible young people who
found themselves relieved of labour for the day and were out for
a good time. As the evening lengthened the brighter grew the
streets with coloured lights, crackers and squibs and, finding
there was no molestation by the police, this continued apace.

'The Salvation Army came out and enlivened the scene with
their spirited music while later the band from Pelaw Colliery
marched into Chester-le-Street and were soon playing martial
airs followed by dance music which many of the young people
were not slow to take advantage of. In one of the broadest parts
of the street those who delight to trip the light fantastic enjoyed
a good time.'

In the evening a short thanksgiving service was held in which the
Rector, Rev. A. de Moleyns, intoned further prayers. The Rev. Enoch
Hall, Congregational Minister, read the lesson and Rev. F.H. Harrison
intoned the prayers. Adjutant Bristow of the Salvation Army was also
present and the Band accompanied the hymns and played the National
Anthem at the close.'

Meanwhile, in Baghdad, George Davison, a brother of **Henderson
Richardson** and **Leonard Sidney Claudian** was composing his
thoughts on the end of the war. He wrote of 'glorious news, joyous
activity, men cheering themselves hoarse and decorum being
forgotten'. Toasts were drunk to, 'the King, the silent navy, our allies
and our dead comrades'. Not only was George the possessor of copper-
plate handwriting but he was a man of some discernment, able to
recognize that he had had an easy and short war and that the private in

Nov 11ᵀᴴ 1918.

HOW GERMANYS CAPITULATION WAS RECIEVED, ABOUT BAGDAD.

I was very glad to get back to my billet, for I was anxious to hear from home, and my letters awaited me. Friday, Saturday and Sunday were full of excitement, and all sorts of rumours were being circulated. In the early hours of Monday evening, we were all restless, for we felt we were about to hear good news. About 9.30 our officer came back from 'Advanced Base' telegraph office, and we needed no word from him, for his face betrayed the glorious news. Germany had capitulated. The village was quiet but not for long. We rang fire alarm bells and gongs, and soon the river front was a scene of joyous activity. Bombs, star-shells, and red, white, and green maroons lit up the sky river and trees. Men cheered themselves hoarse, and with tear-filled

eyes, they shook hands with all and sundry. Arabs who fled, at the demonstration, came back wonderingly, and were ceremoniously shaken hands u by the delighted soldiers. All decor for the moment was forgotten, and officers, men, Indians and Arabs, a fraternised in the hour of trium People hastily scrambled from their beds to join in the rejoicings, and was 2am Tuesday before the final toasts were drank. Everyone in our billet had drink of his own chose and we toasted 'The King', 'our soldie lads', 'the silent navy' 'our loved o at 'home', our 'Allies', and then we rose, and in silence, drank to 'our dead comrades'. One by one, the m sought their beds, tired but happ for we felt, we were at the end of a horrors and soon, we would aga be with our dear ones. Who shal judge a soldier (who has suffered) from going to extremities on suc an occasion, for at last, we had obtained, 'Peace with Victory'.

In conclusion, I may have painted Mesopotamia, in a roseate hue, but I want my readers understand, that they are reading th impressions of a non-combatent. Fur more my rank and profession entitl me to the best of treatment and ac comodation. I came to the country af it had been 'opened out', and suita steps had been taken, to combat i many diseases. My story, would b a remarkable contrast, to any writt by a private in the line. He probably came out, three years fore me, before there were any Y.M.C.A.s canteens, wherein he could buy neccesities. He had to march from place to place, and live out in the open, in a little tent. And he had litt or no chance to receive medical attention. So in conclusion, I wo have you to try and imagine his hardships, and, in return for wha he had suffered, treat him as he deserves.

3ʳᵈ January 1919.

George Davison. C.S.
Army Gymnastic St
Mesopotamia.

George Davison letter.
(Family)

the line had had a much tougher time. He ended, 'I would have you to try to imagine his hardships and, in return for what he has suffered, treat him as he deserves'.

It must have been, indeed, a time of very mixed emotions. The boys were coming home but there were at least 131 widows and 226 children whose husband or fathers were not going to be arriving at the station. How long would it take, if ever, for the inhabitants of Havannah Terrace (fourteen deaths), Nelson Street (fourteen), Castle Street (twelve), Fatfield Square (twelve), Douglas Terrace (eleven), Hobson Terrace (nine), Speculation Place (nine) and Pattinson Town (nine) to emerge from the pall of doom that hung over them?

Now that the war was over the soldiers were gradually demobilized, hoping no doubt to return to the homes fit for heroes, that they had been promised. As is often the case, the high hopes gradually vanished and reality was more likely a quick return to the shifts under and over ground at various collieries and at the iron and chemical works.

Still, for soldiers, there were experiences to be discussed or not discussed, depending on the attitudes and personalities of the now ex-servicemen; one who had an unusual story, and one that he was willing to tell, was Tommy Garnham, a prisoner from April 1915 until the end of the war.

'FATFIELD WAR PRISONER

Corporal Thomas Garnham, DLI, son of Mr and Mrs Garnham, 37 Castle St, Fatfield, enlisted at Birtley as a Territorial at the beginning of the war and was taken prisoner after a six-day sojourn in France, suffering from a broken leg. Since that time his parents have kept him regularly supplied with parcels containing food. The cards and letters sent by him were all couched in similar terms and it was therefore a great delight for them to receive a letter from him saying that he had arrived in Holland and was on his way home. In this letter he was for the first time able to unburden his mind and inform his anxious parents of the terrible ordeal which he had passed through. He states that he was first put to work on a farm and assisted to make roads, clearing land and canal making. Then he was employed on the erection of a large viaduct containing thirty-eight arches. At this time his leg affected him and the doctor told him that he had a diseased bone but such was not the case. The word "coal-mine" he says has quite a different meaning to that in Germany and he speaks of the horrors which our poor prisoners have endured in these places at the hands of cruel masters. A further letter has been received containing the glad news that Corporal Garnham had arrived in Hull on Monday along with other 1,900 from Germany and that he was staying in a convalescent camp in Ripon. He is expected to arrive in Fatfield any day.'

On 7 October 1927, Thomas Garnham, aged twenty seven, was hurt in a fall of stone at Harraton Pit and died a month later, aged thirty-one.

Thomas Garnham – left. (Viv Todd)

Thomas Garnham's watch. (Viv Todd)

Mary Garnham.
(Viv Todd)

A descendant of Tommy Garnham has provided a photograph of him in a German Prisoner of War Camp, wearing wooden clogs but looking reasonably well fed. His wife, Mary, worked for the St John's Ambulance Brigade and her medal is still held by the family. He was awarded a gold watch in 1913, inscribed 'D Comp 8th DLI, Kirkup Trophy won by Private T Garnham. 1913'. It was for rifle shooting.

CHAPTER 12

Homes for Heroes

The June 1914 minutes of Chester-le-Street RDC Housing Committee included details of planned house building and arrangements for prospective tenants of those fifty-seven that had been completed in Usworth. 259 applications had been made and were to be entered into a ballot. Street names for the new houses would be Richardson Terrace, Vernon Street, Viola Street and Dorcas Terrace [all these streets still exist].

Under Part III of the Housing of the Working Classes Act of 1890; the Local Government Board would be approached for a loan of £26,250 for the building of one hundred houses at Harraton Colliery – all to have kitchen, scullery, a bathroom and three bedrooms – and mention was made of the £12,200 already applied for to build forty-seven houses in Washington. (By December, the minutes noted, the price of wood had risen by 25 per cent 'due to war conditions'.)

The war ended any likelihood of these houses being built but in November 1918 the Housing Committee were again discussing forty-seven houses in Washington, one hundred in Harraton and one hundred and twenty-two in Usworth. It was agreed that contracts for building could be advertised and in March 1919 the minutes noted that these schemes had been discussed with the Local Government Board and the Ministry of Reconstruction.

At May's meeting it was noted that there would be only forty-three houses for Washington as a result of more space being given to allotments and gardens. The vacated houses in Birtley, many of the Belgians having gone home, were discussed.

In August it was agreed that the rent for thirty-seven Class A houses would be 7/1d per week and for the ten Class B houses 8/5d per week, as was noted an increase of twenty-five per cent over 1914 prices.

Subsequent meetings give some idea of the complexity of getting the houses built and associated issues. There were, inevitably, disagreements between the council and the various landowners over the price of land, worries over subsidence and discussions re the quotations made by local builders. In short there were some homes and, no doubt, some of them were assigned to men who fitted, by virtue of their service, the classification of 'heroes'.

However, by 1921 there was a general economic depression and as mines were returned to private ownership the miners were locked out, not understanding why their wages ought to be reduced. 1921 saw the lowest coal production figures for any year between 1877 and 1955, with the exception of 1926. Homes for heroes, jobs for heroes?

Homes of Heroes

Wessington U3A War Memorials group has completed the fixing of 94 poppies to houses (or, in a few cases, workplaces) from which men left in 1914 and to which they did not return. Paid for by funds made available through Sunderland City Council's Community Chest and Heritage Lottery Fund the  poppies were designed by Allan Scott, a local sculptor (www.allan-scott-sculpture.co.uk), and fixed by members of the group. Householders have been given a hand painted In Memoriam card with a photograph of the man or his grave (or name on a memorial if he has no known grave).

Before the end of the year, or early in the New Year, there will be leaflets, available from various local sources, for those who'd like to follow the Poppy Walk/Ride around Washington. In addition the group is preparing an HLF funded free phone app for those with smartphones. Starting at Harraton Lodge (or St George's Church for a slightly shorter walk/ride) the route will link the memorials at Fatfield, Washington Village and Usworth Holy Trinity Church. There will be photographs of some of the men, their graves at home or abroad and information about them.

CHAPTER 13

At the Going Down of the Sun ...

In February 1917 Washington Parish Council received a letter from Mr Wanless of Westwood Social Club asking if the council would join the Westwood Club and others to formulate a scheme to provide a memorial to the men of Washington Parish. The council responded that it was already under discussion and that a Roll of Honour was being kept.

In September 1917 WPC agreed to call a public meeting to raise a fund, both to recognize conspicuous bravery and to raise a memorial. The clerk was instructed to write to representatives of F Pit, Glebe Pit, South Biddick Lodges, North Eastern Railway Company, Cook's, Washington Chemicals, the Co-operative Society, clubs, doctors, clergy, teachers, farmers, tradesmen, colliery officials and managers and any others the clerk thought wise to invite. A meeting was arranged for 7 October at 7 pm.

In October 1917 Barmston Parish Council, 'unanimously resolved that it would join Washington Parish Council in collecting funds for the erection of a suitable War Memorial to those from the parishes of Barmston and Washington who have given their lives or otherwise served in the fighting forces' [in the event only the names of the dead were inscribed]. Usworth PC agreed to call a public meeting for 13 October 1917, in the council schools, to discuss a War Memorial and Welcome Home event. A public meeting, held on Washington village green on 24 January 1919, discussed the plans for a War Memorial to be erected on the green. Mr J.H. Mole, the surveyor, explained the plans and, after careful examination of the plans by the councillors, they were approved.

In July 1919 WPC decided to seek permission to build the memorial on the village green and sought permission to move the urinal that was already there. This was carried at October's meeting.

In May 1919 BPC clerk was asked to report about what is 'being done in the parish re Peace Celebrations'. The councillors agreed that they would attend the presentation of a Riley ambulance car to Washington and Barmston War Memorial Committee. The carnival event, costing around £200, took place in August 1919 and photographs of it were featured in *The Illustrated Chronicle* of 4 August. It was organized by the Washington and Usworth branch of Comrades of the Great War and took place at Shafto Terrace Field. Though the photographs are faded, Britannia can be seen on a gun carriage pulled by Boy Scouts and there was a parade of cycles and both fancy dress and tableau competitions. The competitors paraded through Usworth and Washington and judging was carried out by Messrs Ford and Johnson on the carnival field. 'Residents turned out en masse.'

The Washington Area Building Committee, which apparently only operated from October 1919 onwards, and consisted of Messrs Bowser, McBurnie, Mackey, Mansell, Stokoe, Anderson, Burt, Madden, Hall, Hill, Chicken and Rutter, held a special meeting on 31 October 1919. The clerk informed them that he had been in touch with Hugh M. Stobart to get a bowling green as a gift to the Memorial Committee. Mr Stobart was not convinced that the bowling green should be part of the memorial and thought that it was not a good idea to present the finished object or completed scheme but that the committee should raise the money in order that it should be seen as a community facility and achievement. He was prepared to donate £200 to provide the green, labour for its construction or a pavilion; they had three weeks to decide. The council agreed to accept the donation but asked for an extension on the time in order to consult the public.

The first documentary evidence of Harraton's intention to build a war memorial is in the minutes of a Special Parish Meeting in the Schoolroom on 7 February 1917. 'With regard to the recognition of soldiers gaining distinction in the war, it was agreed that the inhabitants of the Parish be asked to honour anyone so distinguished, a public committee to be formed to deal with the question.' The committee then formed consisted of Messrs J. Ainsley, J. Dale, J. Donkin, F. Eley, W. Heslop, W. Kay, W.S. Reeman, J.L. Sanderson, Wm Smirk, Henry Wilson, Jas Wilson and the clerk. Mr Donkin moved that some permanent memorial be fixed to the honour of all who have taken part in the war and this was seconded by Mr Ainsley, unaware, of course, that his son, **George Hedley Ainsley**, would be the first name on the memorial.

There had been a Welcome Home Committee since at least October 1914, Miss Reeman, daughter of the Vicar of St George's, being the leading light. They had no doubt assisted, insofar as they could, the bereaved and the relatives of those men who were away. Concerts and sales of work had been held in order to provide comforts for the troops and to raise money for the presentation of watches for the exceptionally brave.

In April 1918 *The Chester-le-Street Chronicle* reported as follows:

'On Saturday a comic football match was played on the Fatfield Football Ground between the Welcome Home Fund Committees of Fatfield and Pelaw Grange and Brown's Buildings. In the morning a procession was formed composed of many comic characters. These met at the Wheatsheaf Inn, Pelaw Grange and, headed by a mixed band, they proceeded to the Barley Mow and back to Brown's Buildings. From there they journeyed to Portobello, Harraton Colliery and on to Fatfield. They were accompanied by Pompey's tank (kindly lent by the Chester Moor Welcome Home Fund.) Mr T. Watson of 47 Lambton Terrace, Chester le Street, who made this fine model, has been successful up to the present in raising over £50 by exhibiting it in aid of war charities. On this occasion the collection made by the tank was devoted to the Brown's Buildings and Pelaw Grange Fund and the proceeds of the football match were given to the Fatfield Fund. Collections were taken by representatives and Red Cross nurses and various other characters all along the route and also on the football field. There was a large gathering present to watch the comic match, the referee being represented as a police constable who vigorously swung a drum stick and blew his whistle to the diversion of the comic players, who themselves created much mirth by their eccentricities. They were represented by the following characters; Soldiers/sailors, admiral, curate, pierrot, pierrettes, Highlander, Principal Boy, Jew, Janissary, Hussar, coster, Spanish toreador, Colleen Bawn etc etc. The kick off was made by Mr John Todd of the Ferry Boat Inn. The following were the teams -

Fatfield – Goal, Scott - T. Clark, T. Southern, W. Scott, B. Scott, A. Scott, V. Gowland, G. Suddick, G. Elliott, R. Mossman and J. Rodham

Brown's Building – Goal, T. Talbot - J. Gascoygne, W. Younger, J. Green, E. Green, R. Corvie, P. Dalton, A. Sougat, G. Dalton, W. Clark and G. Robson

Referee V. Simpson.

The game was abandoned owing to rain.'

How entirely English, a great day spoiled at the end by the weather.

Harraton Parish Council minutes for November 1918 record that the clerk had been asked to write to the Local Government Board to ask if the council had the power to erect a permanent War Memorial, whether rates could be levied for this purpose and also to cover the cost of the peace celebrations. In December 1918, having had an apparently positive response from the Local Government Board, a committee was set up to supervise the peace celebrations and consisted of Mrs Alexander, Mrs Baker, Mrs Davey, Mrs Kay, Mrs Mason, Mrs McCarton, Mrs Minto, Mrs Oliver, Mrs Renshaw, Mr and Mrs Carr (Harraton), Mr and Mrs Fletcher, Mr and Mrs Sheraton, Mr and Mrs Vince, Mr and Mrs Wood, Mr Donkin and Mr Sanderson.

In February 1919 the council received a deputation from the Harraton Presentation and Memorial Committee and there was discussion about their intention of erecting a stone monument inscribed with the names of the soldiers of the parish. The council agreed to support the idea and agreed to write to the Local Government Board to ask permission for a rate of 2d in the pound to support the scheme.

Meanwhile, in January, the Peace Celebrations Committee had unanimously decided that the peace celebrations would be similar to those for the coronation of George V, i.e. a mug would be presented to all those under fourteen and a cup and saucer to all those over sixty. [Washington also gave out celebration mugs.] The Shiney Row Band and the Fatfield 'Welcome Home Band' would be invited to perform and Birtley Co-operative Society would provide 'ware and cakes' for a tea for the old people in the Fatfield School Hall.

By February 1919, £200 had been raised for the Fatfield Welcome Home Fund and was to be equally divided among the 450 men who had served. A Union Jack banner was made with, on one side, gold letters on an amber and blue background saying 'Honour and respect to our lads that are fighting to uphold the freedom of our empire'.

A deputation from the Welcome Home Committee asked the Parish Council for help with building a memorial of twenty-five feet, on which would be inscribed the names of the fallen. The cost was estimated to be £300, which, it was felt, would not be raised by subscription. The Local Government Board had been approached and had given sanction to levy a rate but they wanted to know the details of the scheme.

In May 1919 the Peace Celebrations committee received quotations for the mugs and cups and saucers. The committee agreed to accept a bid from Hanover Pottery for mugs at 10/6d per dozen and cups and saucers @ 10/6d per dozen.

The parish then had to be divided up to see how many of each item would be needed. The count discovered that there were 1,057 children and 183 old people. It was also agreed that 'afflicted persons' would be allowed to participate. Fifty posters were to be produced to publicize the event and ninety dozen mugs and sixteen dozen cups and saucers were to be purchased.

It was decided that the managers of Birtley and Chester-le-Street Co-ops were to be interviewed before a decision was reached on the catering and a letter was to be written asking if the teachers would supervise the children and arrange the sports events for them.

The two previously mentioned bands were to be asked to offer an estimate of their fees for leading a parade through the village, starting at the bridge at 2 pm and then playing on the green in the evening, at intervals from 5 pm–10 pm. Mr Forster had informed the council that he would be unable to allow the use of the Haggis Hall field, so it was decided to ask Mr Gray, agent to the Earl of Durham, for the use of the football field.

In further meetings in May it was agreed that they would need sixteen waitresses to look after the old people and that the band should start the parade at the bridge at 1.15 pm, play up to the school and then accompany the children and teachers down to the football field and

AT THE GOING DOWN OF THE SUN . . . 133

'there accompany them in their patriotic songs'. It was agreed that the joint tender of the Birtley and Chester-le-Street Co-ops for 1/6d per head for old people and 6½d per bag for the children should be accepted. A surplus of cups and saucers was to be ordered so that any of the committee who wished to buy them could do so. Hanover Pottery then asked the council to pay in advance. There was no chance of that and so the order went to the local Co-operative stores at 9s per dozen for cups and saucers and 12s per dozen for mugs.

In June 1919 the council accepted the tender of £12 from the Shiney Row Silver Prize Brass Band. The event organized for old people was a handicap race, for which suitable prizes were to be given. These turned out to be to the value of £4, a walking stick and a pipe for the two male winners and a shawl and umbrella for the two female winners. Mr Gray said they could use the football field as long as the council would undertake that stock would not be bothered, that there would be no trespassing into adjoining fields and that there would be no damage to fences, hedges or gates; finally, he insisted that there should be no litter left behind.

On 9 July it was decided that, after consultation with Penshaw and Shiney Row Parish Councils, that Fatfield's celebration would be on 19 July 1919. Joseph Cook & Co would be asked to provide for the conveyance of the elderly from North Biddick and Mr Minto, manager of Harraton Colliery, would do the same for the Pelaw Grange elderly.

The Peace Celebrations were duly held with a parade, patriotic songs by children, sports, teas and mementoes. There was dancing in the evening. However, sad to report, 'the prevailing unrest in the country and lack of railway service' meant that the china gifts had not been delivered. Ah well, at least there was peace.

The council, very frugally, sold surplus food for an income of £1.4s.6d and sent thanks to Messrs Sheraton and Vince, respective managers of the Fatfield branches of the Birtley and Chester-le-Street Co-ops. In August, Harraton Council paid £48.12s.2d to Birtley Co-operative Society and £48.8s.2d to Chester-le-Street Co-operative Society for the refreshments supplied.

At the meeting of 28 July 1919 it was decided that tickets would be issued and these could be exchanged for the china gifts at the Primitive Methodist Chapel at Pelaw Grange, the Reading Rooms at Nova Scotia and Cook's Memorial Chapel at North Biddick.

In August 1919 Harraton Council was surprised, and apparently somewhat taken aback, when Washington Parish Council invited them to contribute to presents for the children of Hobson Terrace, Biddick Terrace and The Parade who were due to be entertained in their peace celebrations. Harraton responded, tartly it seems, that, as those children had already been given a day out and a present at the expense of Harraton, there would be no such contribution.

A headline in *The Chester-le-Street Chronicle* on 12 March 1920 read,

'HARRATON PARISH
Generous Gift from Lord Durham
Worm Hill presented to Fatfield
LORD DURHAM PRESENTS WORM HILL
TO THE PARISH'

The article stated that, 'Mr A. Smirk the secretary of the Memorial Fund, informed the meeting of the Parish Council that a deputation had waited upon Mr Gray, agent to Lord Durham, in respect to a piece of land upon which to erect a memorial to the brave boys who had fallen in the great war. He (Mr Smirk) thought it best to lay the matter before the parish meeting. He had received the following letter:

"Lambton Office, Fencehouses
March 2nd 1920

Dear Sir – With reference to the meeting your deputation had with Mr Gray at the Worm Hill, Fatfield, as to acquiring land there for a war memorial and public park, I write to say that Lord Durham will give about 3 acres of land there, including Worm Hill, for this purpose, provided that an undertaking is given that the hill will be preserved and not disfigured or excavated etc and the land fenced off by the controlling authority from Lord Durham's adjoining land. All mines and minerals to be reserved to Lord Durham with full power for winning and working the same, without leaving support and without either himself or his colliery lessees being liable to pay any compensation for damage arising from colliery workings. Will you be so good as to let me know to whom it is desired to have the land conveyed, with full

particulars of names and addresses and occupations and I will ask his lordship's solicitors to have the conveyance prepared – Yours faithfully
Hugh M. Stobart"

'Mr J. Wilson, in moving the acceptance of this letter, said the parish had purchased eighteen gold watches which had been presented to those who had distinguished themselves in action and, to the memory of those who had fallen, it was the intention of the committee to erect a memorial.

'The motion was seconded by Reverend W. Reeman, who expressed his great pleasure to be associated with it. There had been about eighty lads from the parish [actually 102] who had laid down their lives and they ought to thank Lord Durham for presenting this ideal site on which to erect a memorial. Personally, he felt very grateful to his lordship for his generous gift. The motion was carried unanimously.'

A draft of the conveyance of the land was read and approved by the council in May 1920 and in June the conveyance of 2.888 acres of land was signed.

Parish Council minutes included this for 3rd March 1920, 'It was resolved on the motion of Mr Jas Wilson and seconded by Mr W.S. Reeman that the Parish Council be recommended to accept the gift of the Earl of Durham of 2.884 [sic] acres of land comprising the Worm Hill and to grant permission to the Harraton Presentation and Memorial Fund to erect on it a monument as a War Memorial. It was also recommended that the offer of the Fund to hand over the monument, when erected, to the Parish Council be accepted.'

The Illustrated Chronicle was on the case on 22 July, 'Nearly everyone who visits the stately home of Lord Durham and the noble Lambton Park makes a point of pilgrimage to the adjacent Worm Hill at Fatfield, for the little mound is locally historic, in as much as the legendary Lambton Worm is reputed to have coiled itself round this hill at night. Now the mound has come into the limelight through the war, for the Fatfield people, naturally anxious to erect a monument to their sons who made the great sacrifice, have been granted permission by the Earl to erect a monument on its summit.

'The site is an admirable one from the point of view of everybody, except, perhaps, the antiquarians, certain of whom, I hear, are raising their voices in strong protest against the proposal. Their view, however, I understand, will not appreciably affect the intentions of those concerned, but the chances are ultimately that the Worm Hill will not be molested, for an investigation has proved that it is of a very sandy nature and therefore the difficulty of building a good and suitable foundation for the proposed Gothic cross will perhaps necessitate the selection of another site.'

The writer was misinformed because the memorial was built on Worm Hill.

The Chester-le-Street Chronicle of 23 July 1920 was able to supply more details,

'HARRATON'S PROPOSED MEMORIAL

The Harraton Parish War Memorial Committee has decided to erect a handsome monument to perpetuate the memory of the men who fell in the Great War. They have accepted the generous offer of the Earl of Durham to hand over to the Parish Council Worm Hill and upon this site it is proposed to erect the memorial on which the names of the seventy-five [actually 102] men who made the supreme sacrifice will be inscribed. Out of a population of 3,300 in the parish 420 men answered the call, giving a rate of 1.14 per home. The township has recognized [with gold watches] the distinctions so gallantly gained by eighteen of their brave men on the field but they feel that a greater obligation was placed upon them and thus they are appealing to the public to assist them in a laudable object. Mr A. Smirk of Lambton St, Fatfield, is the secretary of the Memorial Fund and will be glad to receive the names and particulars of men whose names are not included in the list received.'

In March 1920 Allan Smirk invited W.H. Wood, an architect in Collingwood St, Newcastle, to design a memorial to be built on the Worm Hill. Mr Wood then put the work out to tender and received quotations from three firms – Alex Pringle, E Bowman and Robert

Beall, the latter being the firm selected. In October 1920 W.H. Wood wrote to Mr Smirk, 'Dear Sir, I had no idea that you were taking me to be a monumental stonemason supplying monuments from stock designs. I only do original designs and obtain estimates from masons for their erection.' The design work done, under this misapprehension, by W.H. Wood had to be paid for but letters in Tyne and Wear Archives suggest that the Presentation Fund was having difficulty paying and so Mr Wood threatened legal action. In 1920 Mr Smirk pointed out that, 'as this is a small place we are having difficulty in raising the amount required' and, in May 1922, Mr Wood's fee still outstanding, asked if it was possible to let it lie over for two to three months. Later, appealing to Mr Wood's altruism, he noted that, 'it is hoped that you will make some reduction as every penny raised is given voluntary [sic]'. Mr Wood could not do that but he did send a donation of two guineas to the Fund. In the meantime the Committee engaged John William Reed, sculptor, of Lodore Road, Newcastle to do the work.

24th Sept 1920

'FATFIELD WAR MEMORIAL

On the occasion of the Flower Show at Fatfield, a tea arranged on behalf of the war memorial was highly successful. The committee collected in Fatfield the sum of £12.9s.3d and at Nova Scotia £6.1s.0d in money and goods. Among those who specially helped were the members of the Fatfield Workmen's Club, Mrs J. Todd (Ferry Boat Inn), Mrs Watson (Dun Cow Inn), and Messrs GW Horner & Co of Chester-le-Street [famous for Dainty Dinah toffee]. A cake given by Mrs F. Nicholson for competition, raised the handsome sum of £5.6s.9d. This, being drawn for, was won by Mrs F. Trelogan of Fatfield. After meeting all expenses the committee had the handsome balance of £43.10s.0d – which they have handed over to the War Memorial Committee. The arrangements were ably carried out by Mesdames F. Nicholson, W. Cumpson, Ainsley, Stangroom, and Marshall, assisted by Messrs A.S. Dean, F. Nicholson, W. Cumpson, J. Ainsley, C. Cumpson and R. Gloyne. The committee – Mesdames F. Nicholson, W. Cumpson, Ainsley, Stangroom, Marshall and Bloomfield and the Misses M. and L. Marshall – desire to thank all in Fatfield and Nova Scotia for their generous support.'

CHAPTER 14

Set in Stone

11 June 1920.

'WAR MEMORIAL
At Washington
UNVEILED BY EARL OF DURHAM

The war memorial of brave men of Washington and Barmston, who fell in the war, and which takes the form of a beautiful Celtic cross erected on the village green at Washington was unveiled by the Earl of Durham last Saturday afternoon. There was a large gathering of the relatives of the fallen, ex-service men, Scouts and the general public. Mark Ford J.P., Blue House, Washington, Head of the Welcome Home and Memorial Committee, presided. The ex-service men and Scouts formed a square on the outside of the cordon, the enclosure being reserved for relatives of the fallen and special visitors. The latter comprised the following: Col. and Mrs Stobart, Col. Ritson, Col. Hawthorne, Col. Turnbull, Col. Henderson, Col. Brereton, Capt Hart, Brigadier-General Durham Light Infantry Territorials, Hon. Cyril Liddle, J. Lawson MP, Coun. Peter Lee, chairman Durham County Council, Coun. W.R. Mole, Chester le Street RDC, Messrs F. Hill, Washington Parish Council, J. Walmsley Usworth Parish Council, WR Potts Barmston Parish Council, Mr T. Trotter representing the Miners' County Executive, Mr Fletcher Smith Durham Mechanics' Executive, Ald. W.M. Smith JP and Mr T. Craggs, members for the district of Durham County Council. Mr W.B. Charlton (Durham Mechanics' Executive) was unable to be present owing to a family bereavement.

Washington Village War Memorial. (Beamish Museum)

THE CEREMONY

The Earl of Durham, having inspected the firing party from the DLI Depot, Newcastle, was invited to unveil the memorial by Mr Mark Ford, who said he hoped the memorial would always help them to realize their responsibilities to the State.

The Earl of Durham remarked that they were there to perform the sacred duty of honouring their gallant dead. No more suitable memorial and no more suitable site could have been chosen. They did honour to the memory of those who fell, and they knew that but for them and their fellow soldiers and sailors throughout the Empire those present would now be victims of Prussian militarism. They won for us that freedom of which we were so proud and for which we would always fight. For the relatives they would always feel the deepest sympathy. "Thank God this county of Durham has done its duty," proceded his lordship. "We may all be proud of the part the county played in the war, and of the sacrifices of its thousands of soldiers and sailors. Today we offer a tribute to the dead. They have not died in vain. We shall ever respect their memories and I hope for hundreds of years this cross will show your children and your children's children what British men can do. I hope everyone who passes this place will look reverently at this monument and will recognize that the true spirit of Englishmen is represented by it. Let us do all we can, determined that we will always maintain England, free, honoured and powerful."

'The memorial having been unveiled, Mrs F.S. Newall laid on the plinth a wreath of arum lilies and laurel, and afterwards wreaths and crosses were placed on the steps by relatives of many whose names appeared on the list of the fallen. Finally, Mrs Mark Ford handed Lord Durham a medal as a souvenir of the occasion and the firing party discharged three volleys prior to the Last Post being sounded. Whilst Lord Durham was inspecting the ex-service men the Usworth band played "Land of Hope and Glory".

THE MONUMENT

'The cross stands on the village green near the main road and the Parish Church. The foundation is circular and of three-tier well-faced concrete, in the centre of which is another five-tier square plinth upon which the cross is mounted. The latter is of "Heworth-blue" artistically designed. The inscription bears the names of 127 men and one woman and reads thus, "Sacred to the memory of those of the parishes of Washington and Barmston who died for King and country – 1914-1919."

'The monument has a back-ground, shaped like a horse-shoe, encircling a clump of tall trees. The enclosure is to be further encircled by the planting of shrubbery in the autumn, to be given by the Earl. This when in bloom will form a veritable umbrella of brilliant foliage overhanging the cross. Hence it is not only most conspicuous to the pedestrian, but very much beautified by its leafy environment.

'Appended are the names of the gentlemen who formed the committee and a summary of the work done: Chairman Mark Ford JP, vice-chairman F.S. Newall JP, S.S. Newall, Major Cook, Rev Cyril Lomax, Rev J.E. Yates, Rev J Young, J.J. Roe, Dr W Jaques, Dr R Farquharson, Ald W.N. Smith JP, treasurer - Mr Jos Ford, secretary - Mr Jas R Carr. The architect was Mr Jos Potts, Eldon Square, Newcastle, with Mr J.W. Reed Lodore Rd, Newcastle, as sculptor.

'After the ceremony, the company adjourned to the schools and partook of light refreshments, and later a tea was provided for the Police and firing squad.'

The memorial included the names of Messrs **William H Borthwick, Alfred Braban, George J. Dobson, Richard Drummond, James E. Dwyer, Robert S. Gould, Joseph Humble, Wallace Layfield, Stephen Mills, Charles Smith, George B. Smith** and **Henry Wilkinson** – all of whom were also commemorated on the Harraton Memorial.

24 February 1922
WAR MEMORIAL UNVEILED AT USWORTH PARISH CHURCH
'A triple commemoration of the men of Usworth who fell in the war was consummated on Saturday with the unveiling and dedication of the very handsome memorial erected in the parish church. A Chancel screen has been provided, and close to has

Usworth War Memorial. (Anne Phillipson)

been put up an alabaster and brass tablet inscribed with the names of the honoured dead. **Lt Alexander James B Begg,** the son of the rector of the parish and Mrs Begg, has a special memorial in the shape of an organ screen, erected by his relatives. On this are painted the cross of the deceased officer's schools and that of his regiment.

'The church was crowded for the ceremony, which was of a most impressive character. The Lord Bishop of Durham, who dedicated the memorials, was supported by the rector of Usworth, Rev. C. Lomax, the rector of Washington, Rev. G.F. Holme, the rector of Penshaw, Rev. T.C. Clayton, the Bishop's secretary, Sir Thos Oliver, Hon Col, Tyneside Scottish, and the churchwardens and Parish Council.

'Mr John Walmsley, chairman of the latter body, unveiled the memorial tablet and Sir Thomas Oliver the organ screen. In doing so, Sir Thomas spoke feelingly of the late **Lt Begg**, who fell on March 21st 1918, serving in France with the Tyneside Scottish, at the age of twenty-one. In him there was cut off a young man of great promise. Educated at Darlington Grammar School and Christ's Hospital, he won a scholarship at Cambridge; but this he never took up, for he joined the Tynesiders the day he left school in 1914. He was wounded in France in 1916 and had not been long back with his regiment when he was awarded the MC for bravery in action. As honorary Colonel of the Regiment, he knew that **Lt Begg** was highly esteemed by General Terman and his brother officers and among them his services in the field were spoken of with appreciation.

'When the Last Post had been sounded by Bugler A. Affleck [his father's name was first on the memorial], the Lord Bishop gave a short address from the pulpit. He spoke of the solemn experiences of the war and the lessons that were to be garnered therefrom. There were four aspects of the war that might be viewed: its natural tragedy, its moral sublimity, spiritual hope and services rendered. The young men who went in the early days to fight against Germany were the nation's best, physically, mentally and morally. In that fearful convulsion of human energy lay the tragedy of the war. On both sides most of the soldiers fought as patriots, serving their country with no selfish motive.

It was disclosed in war-time that man is an amalgamation of the angel and the wild beast: but the angel was more apparent in the tremendous fortitude of the men in the trenches. The services of the war lay in that it made possible what was not possible before, unity among nations, the triumph of law over force, the triumph of democracy.

'The service concluded with the playing of Chopin's Marche Funebre by Mrs Begg at the organ.'

Harraton War Memorial was due to be unveiled in July 1922. Just before that the Parish Council received four tenders for an oak fence to surround the site. They accepted the lowest, £7.5s.0d from Mr Henry Wilson, the same Mr Wilson who had appealed against war service for reasons of business hardship and then, as instructed, found 'work of national importance' at the colliery. Some people had had a better war than others.

24th July 1922 from *The Newcastle Daily Chronicle*
'HARRATON WAR MEMORIAL UNVEILED
'The war memorial which has been erected to commemorate the supreme sacrifice of nearly 100 men of Harraton parish was unveiled at Fatfield on Saturday by Mr Austin Kirkup, chief colliery agent for the Earl of Durham.

'The memorial which has been designed and executed by Mr John W. Reed, sculptor, of Newcastle, is of a handsome appearance and is suitably placed on the Worm Hill.

'At Saturday's ceremony a representative procession was formed in the village, and marched to the site, where the ceremony was impressively performed. The vicar of the parish the Rev. W.S. Reeman and the Reverend C. Wilson and G.W. King (representing the free churches) also participated.

'The Shiney Row Prize Band was in attendance [and was paid £12.0s.0d] and the ceremony was concluded by a firing party and buglers of the DLI from Newcastle Barracks, firing three volleys from sounding the "Last Post". Many handsome floral mementoes, from local organizations and relatives of the fallen, were placed upon the monument.'

The Chester-le-Street Chronicle noted that the inscription was, 'Sacred to the memory of the brave men of Harraton Parish who fell

Harraton War Memorial. (Beamish Museum)

in the Great War 1914-1918.' The paper also quoted fully the comments of Mr Kirkup, who began by apologizing for the absence of Lord Lambton, 'one of the best noblemen in Europe' and then related the story of the Lambton Worm, connecting it to the great struggle in which Lord Lambton's ancestor had fought and slain a kind of terrible tyrant, just as the men of the parish had done at much greater cost. Wreaths were laid by officials of both Harraton and North Biddick Collieries and their respective Miners' Lodges and they were followed by representatives of the churches, the Rechabites, the Good Templars, the Buffs, the Co-op, Fatfield Sports Club, Washington Iron Works, Fatfield Club, Washington Comrades Club, the Memorial Committee and relatives. Proceedings ended with Mr Jeffreys, ex-headmaster of Fatfield School, saying how proud he was of the men he had known as boys and then asking Mr James Wilson, Chairman of the Parish Council to accept the memorial on behalf of the parish. This he did, saying that he expected it would always be treated with reverence and respect and that, when times improved, the parish council intended to create a little park around the memorial.

The event closed with a hymn, three volleys from a firing party from the DLI, the Last Post and the National Anthem.

Newspaper coverage of the unveiling, a close examination of the fabric of the War Memorial and a consideration of other memorials in the village, raise a number of issues. The newspaper listed ninety-seven names (though the text stated there were 120 names) and Mr Donkin announced they had three names to add. In fact they added five names, those of **John R Conlon, George Crichton, Wallace Layfield, George J Dobson** and **James O'Neill.** Careful examination of the memorial shows the depth of incision of the added names to be slightly different. The ninety-seven names on the Memorial are, mostly, the same names as on the plaque in St George's Church except that the plaque has only ninety-three names and does not include **William Armstrong, A Brown, William Culine, George J Dobson, John R. Conlin, Eric Heatherington, Charles Jeffrey, Wallace Layfield, Thomas N. Lonsdale** and **George Crichton.** However the plaque does include Thomas Taylor, a man whose name does not appear on the Fatfield School Memorial, the St George's Roll of Honour or the War Memorial. [In fact, he lived in West Bridge Street, the same street as the **Potter** brothers and is commemorated on Shiney Row War Memorial.]

CHAPTER 15

Epitaph

The Stanley and Chester-le-Street News of 26 October 1922 reported,

'PLAYED QUOITS ON MEMORIAL
Severe Criticism of Alleged Actions at Harraton

Unfortunate occurrences in connection with the local war memorial were referred to at the monthly meeting of the Harraton Parish Council on Wednesday last and the youths of Fatfield village were severely criticized in regard to this.

Coun. James Wilson, the chairman, raised the subject. He said that the council had accepted the charge of the Harraton War Memorial and many complaints had been made that when people went and placed wreaths and flowers on the memorial they were taken off. He thought that, as a council, they might go to the expense of putting up an iron rail about four feet high with a spiked top round the memorial. He thought this would keep the children off.

Coun. Eley alleged it was not the children but the older boys who were the cause of the trouble. He had heard of them stripping the wreaths and using them to play quoits on the top of the memorial. He thought it was the policeman they ought to put on the matter.

Councillor Ray [sic, probably Kay] said it was just what he expected. He referred to the boat house as an example. When that was built the locks were burst open and the boat spiked; whereas had they placed a light in, and some tables and chairs, they would, he alleged, have gone and played cards and guarded it for them (Laughter). They seemed to have a lot of lads in the district who were out for destruction only. They knocked the lamps about shamefully. He moved that they draw the attention of the police to the matter.

Coun. Wilson: If you do that I want you to give him a free hand.

This step was agreed to, the constable to be informed that the council would support him in any prosecution.'

In May 1927 a deputation from the local British Legion approached Harraton Parish Council saying they would like the memorial and its surroundings to be better cared for, more presentable and accessible. The council heard them and agreed to prepare some ideas for the following month's meeting. However, the men from the Legion failed to turn up to the next meeting, which failure led the councillors to agree not to see them without a further appointment. In the event they did receive them, in July, when Mr K. Nash, Chairman of the Legion, asked for metal railings and a locked gate (the key to be kept somewhere handy) and suggested seats at the foot and top of the hill, a path and hand-rail leading up the hill and some flowers to be grown inside the area. The council agreed to give the original war memorial committee a free hand but stipulated that there had to be no excavations and no cost to the council.

In October 1927 the British Legion asked permission to hold a service in November and that was agreed by a vote of five to three. From a modern perspective it is hard to imagine who voted against, and why, especially bearing in mind that all the councillors belonged to families for which the war had meant service for themselves or family members and, in some cases, bereavement.

On 25 November 1928 the War Memorial blew over in a gale and the council found itself discussing what should be done in the way of repairs. Councillor Smirk (Secretary of the original War Memorial Committee) proposed, and Councillor Rodham seconded, that an estimate for repair be sought from a sculptor for making a neat job of the remaining part of the monument without re-erecting the shaft. They agreed that each member would view the memorial prior to the next meeting. In January it was agreed that the damaged column be dressed

Paul Bennett, stonemason.
(Anne Phillipson)

Harraton War Memorial – new cross. (Anne Phillipson)

Harraton War Memorial – job done. (Anne Phillipson)

and re-erected on the die. G.H. Houlding of Penshaw was invited to tender and did so for the February meeting. Unfortunately for him he proposed £15 and Norman Alexander, who had offered to do the work for £10, got the job.

In 2012, thanks to the generous support of Sunderland City Council, a new Celtic cross, designed and sculpted by Paul Bennett of Classic Masonry, was erected on the block. Paul's initials, true to the mason's code, are inscribed where the shaft meets the block – to remain unseen until the memorial is dismantled.

Triple image of Harraton Memorial. (Anne Phillipson)

Washington's schools were closed as the war ended. On 5 May 1919, Mr Goodley of Fatfield School wrote, 'We desire to erect a suitable War Memorial tablet or picture in the Hall, in memory of the thirty old boys and teachers who gave their lives, and in honour of the 100 or more who served in army or navy. Children were asked to subscribe today, and are responding nicely.' The School War Memorial was finally opened on 7 October 1920, 'by J.F. Bell Esq, the Reverend

Fatfield Council School Memorial. (Anne Phillipson)

Reeman presiding. Two teachers and forty-nine old scholars [only forty are actually named on the memorial and one of them was a casualty of the Boer War] are known to have lost their lives in the Great War, and 136 are known to have served in addition. The tablet and roll have cost over £30, raised by subscriptions from scholars, teachers and friends. The County Education Committee have defrayed the cost of framing and glazing the picture, and Mrs White kindly inscribed and ornamented the roll free of charge.

The elder scholars (boys and girls) sang appropriate songs under the musical direction of Mr Stables and the ceremony passed off suitably and successfully.'

There is no indication that other schools commemorated their old boys or teachers but a plaque was erected in Washington Grammar School to Richard Jameson B.Sc. 'sometime Science Master in this school who gave his life for high and pure ideals. 22 December 1917'.

Noo laads an lasses, aa'll haad me pen, cos aa've telt thee aal an aaful story of the brave laads, lasses and bairns of the three parishes of Washington, Usworth and Harraton and the famous First World War.

Addendum

The Heritage Lottery Fund has funded a film/DVD to be first screened on 11 November 2014 at North Biddick Social Club and then made available through YouTube and as a hard copy. The title of the film, which will last around one hour, is 'Washington Men in the Great War – "Wad thou gan? Aye, aa wad."' Using a script by Mark Thorburn of Lonely Tower Films – contact@lonelytower.co.uk – and Peter Welsh and telling the stories of some Washington men, the film has been made with the support of the Durham Pals, Beamish Museum, Durham County Record Office, Biddick School, members of Wessington U3A and some of the relations of the men whose stories are featured.

Further details of the film/DVD will appear on wwmp.weebly.com – the website of Wessington War Memorials Project.

Names on the Usworth Memorial, with Regiment and Date of Death

Joseph Affleck – Northumberland Fusiliers – 1.7.16
Thomas H Alexander – Northumberland Fusiliers – 27.10.18
William Alexander – Durham Light Infantry – 14.12.15
John Askew – Durham Light Infantry – 5.11.16
Joseph Ball – Northumberland Fusiliers – 6.2.16
Fred Balmer – Royal Inniskilling Fusiliers – 8.7.16
Alexander JB Begg – Northumberland Fusiliers – 21.3.18
George Black – Northumberland Fusiliers – 11.4.18
Robert A Bland – Durham Light Infantry – 7.10.16
Richard Boyle – Northumberland Fusiliers – 28.4.17
John Bradshaw – Royal Naval Division – 17.2.17
Michael Brown- Yorkshire Regiment – 22.8.15
William Brown – Royal Naval Division – 20.4.17
Daniel Campbell – Royal Engineers – 23.10.16
R William Clark – Grenadier Guards – 25.9.16
Arthur Cosgrove – Northumberland Fusiliers – 27.3.16
Matthew S Coulson – Royal Marine Light Infantry – 13.7.15
Robert Coulson – Durham Light Infantry – 24.1.16
William Coulson - King's Own Yorkshire Light Infantry – 27.7.17
John Dawson – Durham Light Infantry – 22.7.18
Robert Devlin – Royal Field Artillery – 17.8.18
Matthew Dobson – Royal Engineers – 2.5.18
Alfred E Dodd – Durham Light Infantry – 17.6.19

James Drummond – Northumberland Fusiliers – 1.7.16
Herbert Dunn – Northumberland Fusiliers – 24.4.17
Peter Dunn – Royal Field Artillery – 22.8.15
Liddle B Elliott – Royal Engineers – 8.5.18
Turner Ellison – Royal Field Artillery – 7.10.17 – also on
   Washington
Isaac Ellwood – Royal Naval Division – 4.6.15
George Gibson – Tank Corps – 23.7.18
Joseph Gibson – Northumberland Fusiliers – 18.6.17
George Gouldburn – Border Regiment – 4.2.17
Michael Grafton – Durham Light Infantry – 21.9.14
Thomas Hall – Northumberland Fusiliers – 1.7.16
Matthew Hannah – Durham Light Infantry – 31.7.15
John Harbin – Royal Scots – 27.7.18
Thomas T Hayton – Royal Inniskilling Fusiliers – 1.7.16
James Hepplewhite – East Yorkshire Regiment – 27.9.16
John T Hetherington – East Yorkshire Regiment – 18.6.16
Ralph C Hodgson – King's Own Yorkshire Light Infantry – 27.8.18
Ralph Hopson – Northumberland Fusiliers – 1.7.16 – also on
   Washington
Charles Holland – East Yorkshire Regiment – 22.5.15
John A Hornsby – Royal Engineers – 12.5.17
Collingwood Hunter – Northumberland Hussars – 22.8.18
John M Hunter – Durham Light Infantry – 1.7.16
John P Hutchinson – Lancashire Fusiliers – 11.11.17
Joseph James – Lancashire Fusiliers – 9.10.17
Thomas Jeffrey – Northumberland Fusiliers – 1.7.16
Thomas Johnson – East Yorkshire Regiment – 27.9.15
Archibald J Johnston – Durham Light Infantry - 28.7.16
James Kelly – Durham Light Infantry – 26.3.18
Thomas Kenny – York and Lancaster Regiment – 4.10.18
Austin King – Durham Light Infantry – 17.7.16
John E Lee – Durham Light Infantry – 24.5.16
Thomas Lennon – Durham Light Infantry – 16.9.16
Henry Lewins – Northumberland Fusiliers – 1.7.16
Joseph R Lightburn – Yorkshire Regiment – 5.10.16
Thomas W Lonsdale – Royal Engineers – 17.2.17
Daniel Lowden – Royal Inniskilling Fusiliers – 15.8.15

John Lowes – Durham Light Infantry – 20.1.16
Robert W Lumsden – Machine Gun Corps – 26.7.17
Henry Marriner – Border Regiment – 1.7.16
William Matthews – Yorkshire Regiment – 9.10.17
James H Maughan – Yorkshire Regiment – 5.10.17
Edward McDermott – Northumberland Fusiliers – 5.1.17
John McGivern – Connaught Rangers – 27.11.18
James McTer(n)an – Northumberland Fusiliers – 22.4.18
David Meek – Durham Light Infantry – 21.3.18
George R Meek – Royal Sussex Regiment – 9.4.18
Thomas Morrow – Royal Garrison Artillery – 25.10.18
James H Nesbitt – Yorkshire Regiment – 9.10.17 – also on Washington
Stephen Nesbitt – Royal Garrison Artillery – 26.4.19
Matthew Newton – Durham Light Infantry – 3.3.16
William H Ogle – Northumberland Fusiliers – 28.9.18
Bowman Paterson – Border Regiment – 30.9.18
John G Pearson – Royal Inniskilling Fusiliers – 1.7.16 – also on
    Washington
John Pepper – Northumberland Fusiliers – 30.6.16
Robert Pestell – Durham Light Infantry – 23.10.18
James Postlethwaite – Royal Inniskilling Fusiliers – 15.2.17
Robert J Prest – Durham Light Infantry – 31.3.18
William G Pretsell – King's Own Yorkshire Light Infantry – 20.7.18
John R Punshon – Northumberland Fusiliers – 14.11.16
Richard Purvis – Royal Engineers – 11.5.16
Philip G Ramsey – King's Own Yorkshire Light Infantry – 30.7.17
Richard A Richings – Durham Light Infantry – 7.6.17
William Riddle – Durham Light Infantry – 18.9.16
James Ritchie – Durham Light Infantry – 21.4.16
George Robertson – East Yorkshire Regiment – 16.4.18
James Robinson – Northumberland Fusiliers – 3.7.16
James W Robinson – Durham Light Infantry – 24.6.17
William K Roper – Yorkshire Regiment – 5.7.16 – also on
    Washington
Thomas Sanderson – Northumberland Fusiliers – 28.10.18
Henry Shields – Royal Inniskilling Fusiliers – 1.7.16
Richard Shipley – Northumberland Fusiliers – 16.6.15
John H Simpson – Yorkshire Regiment – 9.4.17

Andrew Smith – Royal Engineers – 15.7.18

Alexander Stephenson – Durham Light Infantry – 7.10.16

James WR Stephenson – Machine Gun Corps – 19.7.17 – also on Washington

William Storey – Royal Engineers – 23.10.19

Henry Tait – Yorkshire Regiment – 6.10.17

William Tappenden – Durham Light Infantry – 10.9.18

Robert Taylor – Royal Garrison Artillery – 13.8.17

Robert W Taylor – Durham Light Infantry – 2.6.17

Usworth Tribute Medal.
(Malcolm and Thelma Smith)

Joseph D Thompson – Northumberland Fusiliers – 10.8.17

John G Thornton – Royal Garrison Artillery – 30.4.18

William Tindale – Northumberland Fusiliers – 17.8.16

Daniel Todd – Northumberland Fusiliers – 19.8.17

Daniel Todd – Northumberland Fusiliers – 6.2.16

John Todd – Dorsetshire Regiment – 12.4.17

Thomas Todd – Royal Irish Fusiliers – 1.7.16

David Trotter – Northumberland Fusiliers – 1.7.16

Joseph Trotter – Royal Engineers – 1.6.16

William Troupe – Royal Inniskilling Fusiliers – 1.7.16

Bertie Walton – Durham Light Infantry – 14.12.15

Matthew Wardle – Army Service Corps – 20.12.17

Arthur C Webb – Royal Naval Division – 17.2.17

William C Webb – Royal Inniskilling Fusiliers – 12.3.18

John Whittaker – Australian Imperial Force – 29.7.17

James W Williams – Durham Light Infantry – 25.3.18

James Wilson – Yorkshire Regiment – 12.5.18

Thomas W Witts – Durham Light Infantry – 9.11.18

Extra information and, often, photographs are available by contacting peterwelshgettysburg@btinternet.com or via wwmp.weebly.com

Names on the Washington Memorial, with Regiment and Date of Death

Thomas Allen – Border Regiment – 29.10.17
John Allsopp – Royal Field Artillery – 3.9.18
Fred Anderson – Royal Field Artillery – 16.11.16
Fred Armstrong – East Yorkshire Regiment – 25.4.18
James Armstrong – Northumberland Fusiliers – 1.7.16
James L Ash – Yorkshire Regiment – 10.7.16
Heatherington Atkinson – Yorkshire Regiment – 22.3.18
Ralph Atkinson – Royal Irish Fusiliers – 1.7.16
Samuel Baggott – Durham Light Infantry – 26.3.18
Charles Baister – Royal Field Artillery – 31.7.17
Charles Ball – Yorkshire Regiment – 18.2.17
William J Ball – Royal Naval Volunteer Reserve – 15.5.17
John Bannister – King's Own Yorkshire Light Infantry – 26.11.18
Joseph Barnabas – East Yorkshire Regiment – 26.9.15
Robert Bateman – Yorkshire Regiment – 17.1.17
Edward Bell – Royal Field Artillery – 12.12.17
Robert Beresford – West Yorkshire Regiment – 22.2.15
Stephenson Besford – Durham Light Infantry – 10.10.15
William H Borthwick – Durham Light Infantry – 7.10.15 – also on Harraton
Alfred Braban – Yorkshire Regiment – 3.10.17 – also on Harraton

AE Braban – not yet identified
Jacob A Branton – Royal Engineers – 30.11.17
George R Brown – Royal Field Artillery – 2.12.17
Robert Brown – Royal Scots – 25.9.15
Walter Brown – Royal Inniskilling Fusiliers – 8.7.16
Walter Brown – Northumberland Fusiliers – 26.10.17
Harry Chilvers – Yorkshire Regiment – 28.9.15
Francis JR Claughan – East Yorkshire Regiment – 10.7.16
John W Cook – Border Regiment – 1.7.16
John Cornish – Yorkshire Regiment – 13.10.16
Joseph Coulthard – Durham Light Infantry – 2.2.16
Thomas Cowell – Durham Light Infantry – 5.1.16
Ernest W Coxon – Royal Naval Volunteer Reserve – 17.10.17
Richard Daglish – Yorkshire Regiment – 10.8.16
George R Davison – East Yorkshire Regiment – 26.9.16
Edward Dean – Durham Light Infantry – 25.7.16
Valentine Dixon – Durham Light Infantry – 28.9.16
Alexander Dobson – Yorkshire Regiment – 17.7.17
George J Dobson – Machine Gun Corps – 18.9.16 – also on Harraton
Thomas Donaldson – Durham Light Infantry – 1.7.16
Patrick Dowd – Yorkshire Regiment – 17.7.17
John Thomas Douglas – Army Service Corps – 30.4.16
Richard Drummond – Yorkshire Regiment – 14.10.15 – also on
   Washington
Francis J Duffy – Yorkshire Regiment – 4.3.16
John R Duffy – Durham Light Infantry – 25.9.15
James E Dwyer – Yorkshire Regiment – 4.5.17 – also on Harraton
John E Ellison – Royal Naval Division – 13.11.16
Turner Ellison – Royal Field Artillery – 7.10.17 – also on Usworth
John W Eltringham – Yorkshire Regiment – 11.1.16
Frank Embleton – Royal Navy – 29.8.18
Matthew English –Durham Light Infantry – 24.3.16
Sarah Ferguson – 23.6.18
Joseph Forster – Royal Garrison Artillery – 2.5.15 – also on Harraton
John D Forster – Dorsetshire Regiment – 18.8.17
George Forster – West Yorkshire Regiment – 16.8.17
William Forster – Yorkshire Regiment – 14.8.16
John T Foster – Durham Light Infantry – 3.10.17 – also on Harraton

Albert V Futers – Durham Light Infantry – 16.9.16
Hugh Gardner – Northumberland Fusiliers – 11.7.16
T Gardner – perhaps DLI – 1.7.16
James Gaston – Royal Army Medical Corps – 5.11.18
John Gilmaney – Royal Irish Fusiliers – 1.7.16
George Golden –Yorkshire Regiment – 21.10.18
Robert S Gould – Lincolnshire Regiment – 9.4.17 – also on Harraton
William Graham – West Yorkshire Regiment - 9.8.15
Robert W Grainge – Royal Scots – 11.8.16
John E Green – Durham Light Infantry – 27.4.15
Edward Hall –Welsh Regiment – 5.11.17
G Norman Hall – East Yorkshire Regiment – 29.9.15
Thomas Hanlon – Royal Fusiliers – 22.8.18
Matthew Harding – Royal Inniskilling Fusiliers – 16.8.17
George W Harrison – Royal West Surrey Regiment – 23.3.18
Joseph Haydock – Army Service Corps – 14.11.18
William Hedley – not yet identified
Edgar Helm – Durham Light Infantry – 1.7.16
Percy Helm – Royal Lancaster Regiment – 20.11.17
Samuel Holbrook – Royal Naval Division – 20.6.15
Thomas Holmes – Border Regiment – 5.7.16
Ralph J Hopson – Northumberland Fusiliers – 1.7.16 – also on
   Usworth
Robert S House – Border Regiment – 26.8.15
George S Huddart – East Yorkshire Regiment – 28.6.17
Joseph Humble – Yorkshire Regiment – 10.7.16 – also on Harraton
Ernest Hunter- West Yorkshire Regiment – 30.8.17
Robert W Ivers – Durham Light Infantry – 9.4.17
Richard Jameson – Royal Welsh Fusiliers – 22.12.17
Robert Jefferson – East Yorkshire Regiment – 15.6.18
Thomas Jefferson – Yorkshire Regiment – 22.8.15
Robert N Jobson – Northumberland Fusiliers – 7.6.17
William Jonas – Middlesex Regiment – 27.7.16
William Knox – Northumberland Fusiliers – 1.7.16
Patrick Lamb – Northumberland Fusiliers – 15.9.16
Frank Lambert – Yorkshire Regiment – 26.9.15
William Lambton – Durham Light Infantry – 14.8.16
Richard O Laws – Durham Light Infantry – 1.7.16

Wallace Layfield – Durham Light Infantry – 24.9.18 – also on
   Harraton
William Lee – Northumberland Fusiliers – 29.3.16
John T Lennox – Coldstream Guards – 22.12.14
Herbert N Lindsay – Northumberland Fusiliers – 4.7.16
Joseph Local – Yorkshire Regiment – 28.9.15
George Lowrie – Royal Engineers – 27.1.16
John A Maddison – Northumberland Fusiliers – 31.3.16
Thomas Mallaburn – Northumberland Fusiliers – 1.7.16
William Marley – Durham Light Infantry – 21.5.16
William J Marley – Manchester Regiment – 9.6.18
Robert Mason – Durham Light Infantry – 26.3.18
William Mason – Durham Light Infantry – 8.10.18
Michael McHugh – Northumberland Fusiliers – 17.6.17
John H McLahaney – Durham Light Infantry – 1.7.16
Henry McMenam – Durham Light Infantry – 27.10.18
Thomas McCrerey – Yorkshire Regiment – 1.7.16
Thomas Megan – Northumberland Fusiliers – 20.9.17
Stephen Mills – Durham Light Infantry – 10.7.16 – also on Harraton
Frederick Morgan – Durham Light Infantry – 14.12.15
Robert Mould – Border Regiment – 23.4.17
Thomas Mould – Durham Light Infantry (Bantams) – 13.2.18
Patrick Murphy – RAF – 15.5.18
James H Nesbitt – Yorkshire Regiment – 9.10.17 – also on Usworth
Robert B Nesbitt – Royal Engineers – 10.10.17
Charles H Nicholson – Yorkshire Regiment – 11.4.17
Harry M Nicholson – Yorkshire Regiment – 26.9.15
Henry J Oswald – Durham Light Infantry – 27.5.18
Harold SG Palmer – Yorkshire Regiment – 7.10.16
Robert Patterson – East Yorkshire Regiment – 25.8.18
Thomas W Paxton – Northumberland Fusiliers – 9.4.17
John G Pearson – Royal Inniskilling Fusiliers – 1.7.16 – also on
   Usworth
Thomas Penaluna – Northumberland Fusiliers – 1.7.16
John R Pittilla – Yorkshire Regiment – 2.4.18
Thomas Pluse – Northumberland Fusiliers – 1.7.16
Joseph W Rawling – Royal Fusiliers – 4.10.18
William Robinson – Durham Light Infantry – 4.12.16

Alfred J Robson – Durham Light Infantry – 26.2.16
John Rooney – Royal Inniskilling Fusiliers – 19.8.16
William K Roper – Yorkshire Regiment – 5.7.16 – also on Usworth
Robert H Ross – Irish Guards – 29.7.17
William K Routledge – Royal Navy – 31.5.16
Ralph Saint – Durham Light Infantry – 11.10.18
Frederick Sandy – Durham Light Infantry – 30.3.18
John T Sandy – Border Regiment – 4.7.16
Thomas Scorer – Royal Navy – 16.9.18
Ernest Seed – Border Regiment – 26.9.15
S Charles Self – Durham Light Infantry – 9.4.18
Ralph T Simm – Yorkshire Regiment – 20.7.16
Henry Simpson – Royal Inniskilling Fusiliers – 1.7.16
Charles H Smith – Yorkshire Regiment – 16.6.16 – also on Harraton
George B Smith – Yorkshire Regiment - 1.7.16 – also on Harraton
John Smith – Yorkshire Regiment – 31.10.18
Joseph Spence – Northumberland Fusiliers – 4.6.16
Joseph Sproul – Yorkshire Regiment – 8.2.17
John F Stafford – Yorkshire Regiment – 12.5.17
Robert Stanners – Royal Field Artillery – 6.6.18
James WR Stephenson – Machine Gun Corps – 19.7.17 – also on
   Usworth
John Stewart – Royal Inniskilling Fusiliers – 29.6.16
William JB Stokoe – Tank Corps – 27.5.18
Joseph E Storey – Yorkshire Regiment – 1.9.15
John Sweeney – Yorkshire Regiment – 7.6.17
John Tatters – Yorkshire Regiment – 2.4.17
Edward Thompson – Durham Light Infantry – 1.10.16
Michael Thompson – Lincolnshire Regiment – 3.6.18
Robert Thompson – East Yorkshire Regiment – 9.5.16
George Tindale – Royal Field Artillery – 19.8.17
John G Todd – Northumberland Fusiliers – 12.3.16
Benjamin Turnbull – Northumberland Fusiliers – 28.10.17
George Urwin – Yorkshire Regiment – 28.9.15
Robert Urwin – Yorkshire Regiment – 20.12.18
Bartholomew R Varley – Army Cyclist Corps – 16.3.16
John Wake – East Yorkshire Regiment – 9.3.16
Marker Wake – East Yorkshire Regiment – 3.10.17

Albert Watson – Durham Light Infantry – 25.10.18
Ernest Watson – Yorkshire Regiment – 9.8.15
Benjamin White – Royal Irish Fusiliers – 22.2.17
Hubert Wilden – Cheshire Regiment – 19.7.16
Alfred Wilkinson – Royal Inniskilling Fusiliers – 1.7.16
Henry Wilkinson – Durham Light Infantry – 26.6.15 – also on
    Harraton
John Wilkinson – King's Liverpool Regiment – 5.8.17
John William Wilkinson – Durham Light Infantry – 19.12.15
Robert Wilkinson – Royal Fusiliers – 18.9.18
Fred Wilson – Northamptonshire Regiment – 13.11.17
Thomas Wiseman – Yorkshire Regiment – 31.12.15
Arthur J Young – Durham Light Infantry – 25.9.15

Washington Tribute Medal. (Edwin Saint)

Names on the Harraton Memorial, with Regiment and Date of Death

George H Ainsley – Durham Light Infantry – 30.10.18
David Anderson – Royal Army Medical Corps – 13.9.17
John G Appleby – Royal Field Artillery – 10.10.15
John T Appleby – Royal Engineers – 9.7.16
Robert Appleby – Manchester Regiment – 23.3.18
William Appleby – Durham Light Infantry (Bantam) – 10.9.16
William Armstrong – Northumberland Fusiliers – 30.4.16
James FG Ashworth – Durham Light Infantry – 25.6.16
John T Bates – Durham Light Infantry – 20.11.18
John A Beer – Yorkshire Regiment – 11.8.15
Richard Bell – Durham Light Infantry – 16.8.17
Francis Blair – East Yorkshire Regiment – 12.3.18
James Bohill – East Yorkshire Regiment – 9.6.17
William H Borthwick – Durham Light Infantry – 7.10.15 – also on
  Washington
JG Bowater – Royal Munster Regiment – 1.5.15 (we think)
Robert Boyle – Royal Inniskilling Fusiliers – 1.7.16
Alfred Braban – Yorkshire Regiment – 3.10.17 – also on Washington
A Brown – not yet identified
Benjamin A Brown – Royal Engineers – 4.10.17
Robert Brown – Dorsetshire Regiment – 29.9.18

John G Charlton – Royal Field Artillery – 4.8.17
Isaac Clark – West Riding Regiment – 17.7.16
Thomas Colpitts – East Yorkshire Regiment – 19.12.15
John R Conlon – Durham Light Infantry – 25.9.15
John T Corps – Royal Irish Rifles – 24.8.18
George Crichton – Northumberland Fusiliers – 10.2.15
Newrick Crow – Northumberland Fusiliers – 18.9.16
Ralph Crow – Northumberland Fusiliers – 6.9.16
Thomas Crow – Northumberland Fusiliers – 26.10.17
William Culine – Durham Light Infantry – 12.4.18
Joseph Cumpson – West Yorkshire Regiment – 26.9.16
Leonard S C Davison – Durham Light Infantry – 5.10.17
Henderson R Davison – Royal Engineers – 1.10.18
Samuel Dawson – Durham Light Infantry – 2.4.18
Benjamin Dean – Machine Gun Corps – 21.9.18
George J Dobson – Machine Gun Corps – 18.9.16 – also on
    Washington
Benjamin Doyle – Northumberland Fusiliers – 1.7.16
Richard Drummond – Yorkshire Regiment – 14.10.15 – also on
    Washington
John Dunn – Royal Irish Regiment – 19.10.14
William T Dunn – Royal Field Artillery – 23.1.18
James E Dwyer – Yorkshire Regiment – 4.5.17 – also on Washington
Jacob Emery – Durham Light Infantry – 21.5.16
Henry Fletcher – Yorkshire Regiment – 1.7.16
John Thomas Forster – Durham Light Infantry – 3.10.17
Edward Foster – Durham Light Infantry – 16.9.16
Thomas Foster – Northumberland Fusiliers – 1.7.16
Michael Gibbons – Royal Field Artillery – 9.10.16
Richard Gloyne – Durham Light Infantry – 21.9.17
Robert S Gould – Lincolnshire Regiment – 9.4.17 – also on Washington
Matthew Grass – King's Own Yorkshire Light Infantry – 8.10.18
Edward Hall – East Yorkshire Regiment – 9.8.15
Eric Heatherington – Royal Warwickshire Regiment – 4.5.17
Philip Hope – Royal Field Artillery – 1.11.18
Joseph Humble – Yorkshire Regiment – 10.7.16 – also on
    Washington
W Hunter – not yet identified

Charles Jeffrey – Northumberland Fusiliers – 1.7.16
George Johnson – Durham Light Infantry – 5.8.17
Michael Kelly – Yorkshire Regiment – 12.1.17
Arthur Kirton – Durham Light Infantry – 19.12.16
John W Kirton – West Yorkshire Regiment – 14.7.16
Joseph Laverty – Royal Garrison Artillery – 5.8.17
Wallace Layfield – Durham Light Infantry – 24.9.18 – also on
   Washington
James Leslie – Black Watch – 20.9.15
Thomas N Lonsdale – Lancashire Fusiliers – 5.10.18
Nathan Marshall – Royal Army Medical Corps – 20.8.16
Robert Marshall – Northumberland Fusiliers – 11.4.18
William G Mawson – Durham Light Infantry – 22.9.16
William McCulloch – Royal Army Service Corps – 12.5.16
Lawrence McKeon – Loyal North Lancashire Regiment – 5.9.18
Ralph McNeil – Royal Field Artillery – 22.4.17
John McNeil – Durham Light Infantry – 19.12.15
Alexander J Metcalfe – Durham Light Infantry – 27.7.16
Stephen Mills – Durham Light Infantry – 10.7.16 – also on Washington
William Moore – Durham Light Infantry – 27.8.17
Hugh Murray – East Yorkshire Regiment – 9.9.15
Thomas Nattrass – East Yorkshire Regiment – 1.1.17
James Nicholson – Northumberland Fusiliers – 1.7.16
Fred Nicholson – West Yorkshire Regiment – 11.5.17
John W Noble – Royal Scots – 23.11.17
James G Oliver – Royal Inniskilling Fusiliers – 1.7.16
Thomas Oliver – Durham Light Infantry – 1.10.16
 James O'Neill – Durham Light Infantry – 21.10.17
Alfred H Potter – Yorkshire Regiment – 4.8.16
John F Potter – Durham Light Infantry – 10.9.18
Robert Richardson – Yorkshire Regiment – 27.9.16
John Ross – Lincolnshire Regiment – 18.6.18
Herbert Scott – Northumberland Fusiliers – 4.7.16
Charles H Smith – Yorkshire Regiment – 16.6.16 – also on Washington
Charles Smith – Royal Naval Division – 22.12.17
Ernest Smith – Royal Warwickshire Regiment – 7.9.17
George B Smith – Yorkshire Regiment – 1.7.16 – also on Washington
Robert W Syson – West Yorkshire Regiment – 10.10.17

George A Thompson – Lincolnshire Regiment – 14.8.17
Charles Todd – Royal Field Artillery – 6.8.15
George Usher – Durham Light Infantry – 27.10.18
Thomas Walker – Northumberland Fusiliers – 1.7.16
Charles Watson – Royal Veterinary Corps – 16.11.16
Henry Wells – Northumberland Fusiliers – 1.7.16
John Whitfield – Royal Garrison Artillery – 4.11.18
William Whitfield – Durham Light Infantry – 21.9.16
Henry Wilkinson – Durham Light Infantry – 26.6.15 – also on
  Washington
Robert Willis – Durham Light Infantry – 1.7.16

*John G. Charlton's inscribed watch
case. (Dot Short)*

There are 121 names on the Usworth Memoral, 179 on the Washington
Memorial, and 102 on the Harraton Memorial. However, of these 402
names, nineteen men – **Turner Ellison** – Royal Naval Division; **Ralph J.
Hopson** – Northumberland Fusiliers; **James H. Nesbitt, William K.
Roper, James E. Dwyer, Charles H. Smith, George B. Smith, Joseph
Humble, Richard Drummond and Alfred Braban** – all Yorkshire
Regiment; **John G. Pearson** – Royal Inniskilling Fusiliers; **Robert S.
Gould** – Lincolnshire Regiment, **James W.R. Stephenson** and **George
J. Dobson** – Machine Gun Corps; **William H. Borthwick, Wallace
Layfield, Stephen Mills, John T. Forster** and **Henry Wilkinson** – all
Durham Light Infantry, are named on two memorials.

Index

All soldiers and sailors who were **killed** or **died** in the war and are mentioned in the text are listed in this index and have their names **emboldened**.

Accidents in pits, 46
Affleck, A., 143
Ainsley, George H., 107–108
Alexander, Norman, 151
Allotments, 22, 87, 126
   at Fatfield Council School, 92
Appleby, John G., 46-7
Apples, theft of, 103
Armstrong, Fred, 111-12
Armstrong-Whitworth, 60–1, 80
Ashworth, James F.G., 23

Bairnsfather, Bruce (Old Bill),
   102
Barmston Parish Council, 22, 87,
   104, 128
Begg, Alexander J.B., 143
Belgians, 26, 44, 56
   in Birtley 80–3
Bennett, Paul (Classic Masonry),
   149, 151
Birtley Co-op, 17–18, 20, 132
Birtley Iron Co, 43
Blackberrying, 92
Bloomfield family, 35, 137
Bottoms, W. (Councillor), 21, 35
Bravery *see* Medal presentations

British-American fellowship, 80
Butchers, pork, 25

Charlton, John G., 118, 167
Chester-le-Street Co-op, 19, 119,
   132–3
Chester-le-Street Rural District
   Council, 13, 21, 80, 82, 85,
   103
Chicken, E.W., 114
Children, 15, 19–20, 50, 57, 88–
   92, 101, 123, 133–4, 152
Christmas, 16, 18–20, 22, 26, 40,
   55, 101, 119
Cigarettes, 26, 28, 33
Claughan, Francis J.R., 114
Coal Mines:
   F Pit, 10, 15, 22, 31–2, 128
   Glebe, 15, 22, 128
   Harraton Colliery, 11, 13, 15,
      45, 126, 133, 146
   North Biddick Colliery, 12–13,
      15, 21, 24, 118, 146
   Springwell, 14
   Usworth Colliery, 14–15, 21,
      27
Collette, E.M., 113–14

Conscription, 42
Conscientious objection, 43–4
Cook's ironworks, 10, 91–3,
    128, 133
    employees at – **Alfred
    Braban, Richard
    Drummond, Robert S.
    Gould, Stephen Mills, John
    F. Potter, Charles Smith,
    George B. Smith**
Cox Green footbridge, 21
Crichton, George, 32–3, 146
Cricketers, England, 24
Cross Keys public house, 21

Dent, Robert A., 118
Dr Cassell's tablets, 53
Dainty Dinah toffees, 55–6, 137
Davison, George, 99, 121–2
Davison, Leonard S.C., 99,
    121
Davison, Henderson R., 99,
    121
Defence of the Realm Act
    (DORA), 41–2, 55, 85, 103
Douglas, John T., 68
Drummond, Richard, 49–51,
    92
Dunn(e), John, 32
Dunn, William T., 45
Durham Football Association, 23
Durham Miners' Gala, 14

Elliott, Liddle, 17
Elliott, Liddle B., 17
End of the war, 116, 119, 121,
    123
England cricketers, 24

Estell, Sidney, 43–4

Fatfield Bridge, 14, 40–2
Fatfield Mothers' Union, 28
Fatfield Sisterhood, 28
Ferguson, Sarah, 111
Ferryboat Inn (Toddy's), 66–7,
    76
Films, 25
Food supplies:
    and recipes, 57, 84–5
    fish – the lack of in the River
        Wear, 104–105
    potatoes, 104
    see also allotments
Football, 23–4, 56, 65, 74–6, 130
Ford Mark J.P., 129, 138, 140–1
Futers, Albert V., 67
Futers, Stephen R., 67

Gallipoli, 8, 40, 42, 46–8, 97
Garnham, Thomas, 123–5
Germans in Washington, 25–6
Goodley, Mr (headmaster of
    Fatfield School), 23, 91, 152
Grafton, Michael, 29
Guy, Martin, 68

Hall, Reverend Enoch, 20, 122
Hanlon, John, 114
Harraton Parish Council, 13, 20,
    52, 58, 67, 87, 115, 131, 134,
    136, 147–8
Hartlepool, 34, 50
Holbrook, Samuel, 48
Holmes, Reverend, 22, 25
Housing, 28, 123, 126–7
Hume, Grace, 25–6

Jack and Tommy's bairns, 26, 101
Jameson, Richard, 153
Johnasson, Gordon and Co., 14
Jonas, William, 24, 74–6
Jutland, Battle of, 70

Kelly, Michael, 25
Kelly's Directory, 10–11, 13–14
Kirkup, Austin, 13, 21, 88, 117–18, 144, 146

Lambton and Hetton Coal Co., 13, 21
Lambton Worm, 11, 22, 135, 146, 153
Laverty family, 35
Laverty, Joseph, 35
Layfield, Wallace, 45
Lennox, John T., 31–2
Lindsay, Herbert N., 107
Lomax, Reverend, 35, 94, 141, 143
Lomax, Mrs, 57
Loos, Battle of, 49–50, 54, 65, 113
  casualties at - **James Leslie, John R. Conlon, John R. Duffy, Frank Lambert, Joseph Local, Harry M. Nicholson, Arthur Young, Joseph Barnabas, Robert Brown, Harry Chilvers, George Urwin**

Marsden, Sergeant, 66
Marshall, Nathan, 43
Mawson, George W., 36–7

Medal presentations, 106, 113–18, 143
Memorials:
  Begg, Alexander J.B., 143
  Fatfield Council School Memorial, 152–3
  F Pit, 31–2
  Harraton St George's Roll of Honour, 67, 92, 118, 146
  Harraton Parish War Memorial, 129–37
  Jameson, Richard, 153
  Thiepval, 72
  Usworth Memorial, 141–4
  Washington Roll of Honour, 67, 69, 128
  Washington Village Memorial, 128–9, 138–41
Metcalfe, Alexander J., 23
Minto, G.W., 11, 13, 60, 116–17, 133
Minto, Oswald, 117
Moore, William, 118
Mossman, George, 116–17
Mourning, ready to wear, 53
Mulvey, Patrick, 113
Munitionettes, 61–3
Murphy, Patrick, 101, 109–11
Murray, Hugh (Morrow), 48–9

National Egg Collection, 91
Nattrass, Thomas, 46, 94–8
Neal family, 34–5
Nelson, Captain G.S., 115–16
Nicholson, Fred, 45

Old Bill (Bruce Bairnsfather), 102

O'Neill, James, 100–101
Opposition to war, 46

Parish magazine (Washington
  Holy Trinity), 32, 69–70, 94
Patterson, James, 94
Peace celebrations, 120, 129,
  131–4
  in Chester-le-Street, 119–20
Penaluna, Thomas, 94
Pensions, 60–1, 72, 112
Pigeons, 20
Poppies, 127
Pork butchers, 25
Potter, Alfred H., 106–107
Potter, John F., 105–106
Prince of Wales' Relief Fund, 17,
  24, 65, 89, 91
Profiteering, 102–103

Recruiting, 22, 24, 27, 38–9
Reed, John William, sculptor,
  137, 141, 144
Reeman, Reverend, 11, 115, 130,
  135, 144
Reeman, Miss, 28, 130
Robinson, L.C., 116
Robinson, William, 78
Robson, Alfred J., 69
Sailors,
**William J. Ball, Ernest W.
  Coxon, Frank Embleton,
  Thomas Scorer, William C.
  Routledge,** 70
Scavengers, 21
Scorer, Thomas, 70, 107
Scott, Herbert, 72–3
School strike, 88–91

Seagar, J.F., 118
Shirkers (and Weary Willies), 26
Shops *see* Washington, shops in
Simpson, W., 114
Smirk, Allan, 134, 136–7
Somme, Battle of, 71–2, 74–6
  casualties on 1st July: **Joseph
  Affleck, James Drummond,
  Thomas Hall, Thomas
  Hayton, John M. Hunter,
  Thomas Jeffrey, Henry
  Lewins, Henry Marriner,
  John G. Pepper, Henry
  Shields, Thomas Todd, David
  Trotter, William Troupe,
  Thomas Mallaburn, James
  Armstrong, John H.
  McLahaney, Thomas
  McCrerey, John G.
  Pearson, Thomas Penaluna,
  Thomas Pluse, Henry
  Simpson, George B. Smith,
  Alfred Wilkinson, Ralph
  Atkinson, John W. Cook,
  John Gilmaney, Edgar Helm,
  Ralph J. Hopson, Richard O.
  Laws, Thomas Donaldson,
  Robert Boyle, James
  Nicholson, James G. Oliver,
  Thomas Walker, Henry
  Wells, Robert Willis, Charles
  Jeffrey, Thomas Foster,
  Henry Fletcher, Benjamin
  Doyle**
Stobart, H.M., 129, 134–5, 138
Stobart, Mrs, 58
Tatters, John, 94
Taylor, Robert W., 50

Thomas, R.C., 118
Todd, Charles, 52–3, 67
Todd, John G., 69
Tribunals, 42–5
Tribute medals, 157, 163

USA joins the war, 79–80
Usworth and Springwell Red
   Cross Guild, 28
Usworth Holy Trinity Church, 8,
   14, 50, 127

Varley, Bartholomew R., 69
Visits to the wounded, 49

Wake, John, 69
War Memorials *see* Memorials
Washington Chemicals, 10–11,
   21–2, 87, 91, 123, 128
Washington and District
   Volunteer Record, 27, 29, 31,
   53
Washington Holy Trinity
   Church, 10, 35, 57, 107
Washington Station Methodist
   Church Brotherhood, 35
   casualties from, **Thomas
      Allen, Charles Ball, Robert
      Bateman, John E. Green,
      Thomas Paxton, John R.
      Pittilla, Ernest Seed, John
      Smith, Joseph Sproul,**

**Benjamin White, Fred
   Wilson,** 35
Walter, Willson, 17
Washington, shops in, 10–12,
   17–19, 25, 90
   see also Birtley Co-op
   Chester-le-Street Co-op
Watson, James, 114
Weary Willies (and shirkers), 26
Wessington U3A, 127
Whittaker, John, 101
Wilkinson, Henry, 52
Willcocks, Thomas, 76–7
Wiseman, Charles (Councillor),
   22
Wiseman, Thomas, 22, 53–4
Women:
   Armstrong-Whitworth's, 59–
      60
   Fatfield Sisterhood, 58
   Fatfield Mothers' Union, 28
   Holy Trinity Washington
      Ladies, 57
   Munitionettes, 61–3
   Women's War Agricultural
      Committee, 58
Worm Hill, 11, 134–6, 144
Wormhill Terrace, 12, 87
Worm (Lambton), 11, 22, 135,
   146, 153